Refine & Grow

Lessons Learned on Navigating
the Business World

Refine & Grow

Lessons Learned on Navigating
the Business World

Lynse Allen

BUSINESS
BOOKS

Winchester, UK
Washington, USA

JOHN HUNT PUBLISHING

First published by Business Books, 2023
Business Books is an imprint of John Hunt Publishing Ltd., No. 3 East St., Alresford,
Hampshire SO24 9EE, UK
office@jhpbooks.com
www.johnhuntpublishing.com
www.johnhuntpublishing.com/business-books

For distributor details and how to order please visit the 'Ordering' section on our website.

A CIP catalogue record for this book is available from the British Library.

Design: Matthew Greenfield

UK: Printed and bound by CPI Group (UK) Ltd, Croydon, CR0 4YY
Printed in North America by CPI GPS partners

We operate a distinctive and ethical publishing philosophy in
all areas of our business, from our global network of authors to
production and worldwide distribution.

Contents

To anyone who has ever served in the role of mentor,

Thank you for your patience, wisdom, desire for improvement, and willingness to teach. By sharing your knowledge, you helped shape the definition of success for others. Through them, your lessons will continue to impact and inspire future generations.

Acknowledgments

My primary mentors, Shanae Strayer and Justin Uhler, were responsible for teaching me many of the lessons outlined in this book. Without their direction and leadership, I would not have known the feeling of building a career I could be proud of. I know for certain this book would not exist without them. I must thank my friend, Leah Kayajanian, who encouraged me to pursue my dream, offered to be my editor, and coached me on the art of writing. I also need to thank my brother-in-law, Dustin Mack, and cousin, T.J. Kasperbauer, who are published authors, and helped shepherd me through the process. Of course, I must thank my husband, Mike. He enthusiastically supported my decision to pause my career and take time off to write a book even though I had never written anything before. Nobody has ever supported me like he does. In addition, the curiosity and innocence of our 4-year-old daughter, Josslyn Ann, fed my desire to be better and dream bigger every day. Finally, to the numerous professors, colleagues, clients, stakeholders, and team members I have learned from and worked with, I was fortunate to have crossed paths with you. Some of you shared nuggets of wisdom that present themselves in this book. Others taught me what not to do, which was an equally powerful lesson. Most importantly, I have an appreciation for you, the reader, for deciding to be open-minded and following a desire to progress and develop yourself. I, too, sought and continue to seek ways to evolve. I know the struggle of working day-in and day-out and feeling overwhelmed, underappreciated, and unsure of how to improve the situation. I feel deeply grateful to have achieved my dream of publishing this book and hope that my broader goal of helping others will also be realized. I am humbled to know this book would not exist if not for the intuition, intellect, support, and confidence of others.

Introduction

This book came to fruition over the course of a decade. It started by my taking notes on advice I was getting from managers at my consulting firm. I jotted down any important tips they had on how to navigate my career successfully. At the time, I worked for a company that thought it was of utmost importance to invest in the development of their people. I gained incredible insight from working day-in and day-out with a large group of professionals whose goal was to develop and teach me. As I grew my network within this company, I learned more and more, and found that I had filled up entire spiral notebooks with commentaries about how to approach different business personalities, problems, and unforeseen circumstances. It got to the point where I thought, *there are so many great tidbits, I could write a book*. My thinking evolved into *I should write a book*, until finally, I wrote the book. In what I can only describe as an incredible stroke of luck, I crossed paths with a couple of the wisest managers first, and they became mentors early on in my career as a management consultant. I was taken aback by how differently they saw solutions and the unconventional path they recommended I follow to achieve success. They advocated for unplugging from work every single day, and identifying periods of time that I was completely unavailable. They told me that sitting in silence is powerful and that I can take up to 3 days to respond to non-urgent emails. They told me I couldn't have more than three priorities at one time and that I should expect to fail – a lot, but that I would build a strong reputation anyway. My instinct was to reject the path they outlined, as it did not conform to what I interpreted as the rules for success. It did not focus on verbal recognition, moving up quickly, ensuring others acknowledged and were aware of my attendance in meetings, or aiming to be seen as a hard worker who can take on

1

and balance many books of work all at once. I blindly followed their guidance, mostly to feed my curiosity. I wanted to conduct my own quasi-experiment and determine if the advice they offered could work. When it did, I began my journey to unlearn what I thought was the path to success. Then, I wanted more. I asked my mentors to share workplace guidance and advice on anything and everything they could think of. I wanted to acquire as much knowledge as possible. I wrote my experiences down and continued to keep notes on what these mentors said, as well as my own observations about why and how the advice worked.

As I moved up the hierarchy of my corporate career, I started to have direct reports and mentees of my own. I passed the lessons from my mentors down to them. What struck me was that they shared my initial reaction. When I told them how unplugging from work makes you better, awkward silence is an opportunity and tool, some work time should be devoted solely to pondering problems and solutions, some things on your plate can only be given a C-level effort, and in many circumstances, it's better to say no than yes, their first instincts were to question, and sometimes even snub, this advice. Those who ignored their predispositions and tried a different way had the same experience I did. That was when I realized these were lessons that needed to be shared on a broader level. I knew that many people approached their career and the path to achievement using the same ideas I initially thought would prove successful – those who are loyal, dedicated, and dependable employees are always available, if a long silence occurs in a conversation, then you fill it to avoid awkwardness, thinking about something does not equate to work time, always give an A+ level in everything you do, and always say yes. That meant many people could benefit from changing their perspective and learning more about the path that was shown to me – a path that explained how to think about and approach problems and solutions in a different way.

I also noticed that a cyclical pattern emerged as I continued to evolve my skillset. During times when I blindly followed the advice of my mentors, I experienced immense growth. Each piece of guidance took practice and focus to fully absorb and implement into my daily routine. When I was learning how to use and apply the skills for the first time, it felt awkward and sometimes painful because I had stepped out of my comfort zone. Once I grew into the new approach my mentors taught me, I would go through the next phase: refining my approach. I made small, iterative improvements until I felt a shift. I had moved from practicing to perfecting and, finally, to being the expert. Inevitably, a new and different problem would present itself. Again, I would ask my mentors for advice, be taken aback by the recommended approach, and re-enter a growth cycle. I noticed the pattern was true for organizations as well – they would experience rapid change and growth cycles, then pause for refinement and iterative improvements. This realization is how I determined the name of my business and this book. I wanted people to recognize that these cycles we all go through – as individual employees and as team members of an organization – are the phases required to evolve. First grow each skill, then refine it to achieve your goals. When an organization goes through growth, be flexible and recognize you can't control or change it. When the change or growth cycle subsides, then adopt and accept that new technology, re-structure, or expectation of how to do things – you will thrive by adjusting and perfecting your approach to meet the latest needs of your managers and customers.

I decided the best way to reach a wider audience was through turning my spiral notebooks into a book that could explain how to acquire and apply these soft skills, so anyone who wanted could learn new tips and better ways to navigate their business careers. I initially identified my target audience as entry-level employees and graduate students studying business or liberal arts, with an intent to work in a corporate setting. I thought it best to position this book as a supplemental textbook that could provide guidance to students on how to interpret and navigate the corporate world before they even entered it. However, in the process of writing the book I realized that although the book is vital to the student and entry-level audience; it is most applicable to people who are already navigating the business world. Whether they are doing this successfully or not, what matters most is that they seek new ideas and suggestions in terms of how to achieve work-life health, do more with less, build better relationships, and establish a solid reputation.

The principal audience is management consultants and middle to upper management employees, particularly those who work with and for Fortune 500 companies. That is the audience who will best relate to my journey, examples, and scenarios – because they are *currently* experiencing them. This audience can be expanded to lower-level executives, employees of mid-size technology and software companies, non-management consulting vendors who contract with large corporations, as well as upper to middle management employees who work in diverse industries – including healthcare, government, and non-profit sectors. Regardless of industry or organizational level, the best reader is someone who is looking for techniques and strategies that will set them apart from their colleagues and enable their path to promotion as leaders and executives within their company or industry. Although the book was written primarily as a "how to" guide for these audiences, I have since realized these lessons can be applied to most any type of career, and in many cases, to personal life scenarios as well. I introduced many of the lessons into my personal life and found that they helped me to become more thoughtful, present, and focused.

The traits and motivation of the consumer of this content are key. The ideal reader is someone who sees value in building their skillset in order to pursue a career path that gives them purpose, and wants to make the organization they work for better. Your goal should always be to leave an organization better than you found it. This is the concept behind adding value. For every lesson written in this book, the primary goal is to teach someone how to add value. This was one of a few basic principles from which the book was written. In addition, you must feel that the career path you've chosen aligns to what you feel compelled to do, or have a deep interest in. If you're in a role that you feel no passion for and read this book, it won't be nearly as useful. The assumption is that you want to be successful and are looking for opportunities to improve. If this isn't the case, then the first step is to find a new career that aligns with your motivation and goals. The final assumption this book makes is that you care deeply about your reputation. In order to digest and try out these new strategies, you must desire to build a strong and respectable reputation. For the purposes of this book, that means you already have, or intend to build, an awareness about how you've been perceived by colleagues, leadership, and stakeholders in terms of willingness to get to a solution, ability to collaborate and work well with others, and the ideas and suggestions you bring to the table.

It is important for me to note this book doesn't focus on managing and motivating others. I focus on intrapersonal soft skills and coaching you on how you, yourself, can do and be better, not how you can teach others to. I acquired these lessons throughout the early years of my career as a management consultant and much of what I learned was in a large, global, corporate setting. For simplification, I make note of how to apply examples to other roles and clarify consulting verbiage and corporate terminology, both in the chapter and in the glossary at the end of the book. Every chapter title is named after a piece of advice I received from a mentor. While the context within each chapter is aimed at how to take that advice and incorporate it into a day-to-day routine, there are also several other anecdotes included to help frame the overall story. I sprinkled these themes and additional guidance throughout all chapters. I included a summary of advice and strategies for implementing the overarching lesson at the end of each chapter. Some tactics I introduce early on in the book are referenced in later chapters. The intention is for you to build off your knowledge base as you progress through the book. My recommendation is to read the entire book from front to end first, then go back and revisit chapters that outline the skill you want to prioritize. Once you master that first skill you feel could be most transformative to your current circumstance, you can introduce the next piece of advice. Repeat this until you've grown into all the pieces of advice, refined them to your liking, and folded them into your daily routine.

I wrote this book because it aligned with my desire to help others and my passion for teaching. I majored in psychology in college because my goal was to become a therapist. I thought that was the best way to help others – to teach them how to do and be better. Halfway through my studies, I realized I could reach more people if I shifted my focus to organizational psychology. That was a way to help thousands of people at a time. I could teach companies how to set up and enforce positive working environments so that their people could flourish. I could coach people and help them navigate their work life. I realized that would be even more impactful because most people spend 40+ hours per week, over 40+ years of their lives, at work. I thought if people spend the majority of their lives at work, it should be something they enjoy. I want to help people feel excited about waking up and getting to work. I don't want them to feel like they are in a rut with their career, or unhappy and discouraged day-in and day-out. I want employees to avoid spending every week waiting for the weekend to arrive. And ultimately, I want people to look forward to their growth cycles and see the opportunity they have to forge a career path they can be proud of.

When I began the writing process, I identified some parameters as the foundation for writing this book. Specifically, I defined what it would and would not cover. While I defined each lesson, or chapter, outlined here as "soft skills," the term itself covers a broad list of traits, only some of which this book focuses on. However, it is the correct term to describe the intangible and intrapersonal skillsets that I provide guidance on. One book with a couple hundred pages cannot realistically encompass every aspect and type of soft skill. The softs skills captured here focus on how to build a strong reputation within a company, learn and sort complex information quickly, frame conversations to get better data and explanations, adjust personal approaches and communication styles to build better relationships, think strategically and see the whole picture, and most importantly, learn how to add the most value to an organization.

One of the best things I did in my career was to buy-in to the idea that I needed mentors to help guide me through. While I chose not to create a chapter specific to this important aspect of building a career, each chapter I wrote tells the story of how a mentor or colleague I respected passed their wisdom on to me. If there is only one thing gained from reading this book, my hope is that you, the reader, seek out mentors who emulate what you aspire to be and have achieved what you hope to accomplish someday. When picking mentors, focus on quality over quantity. As you'll notice while you read, I focus on two mentors in particular, and I only needed those two to come up with hundreds of lessons over the course of the last decade. Most importantly, be open to trying something in a new way. If you feel stuck in old habits and ways of thinking, but refuse to grow by trying something new, you cannot expect to see a different result. Anytime I felt stuck, it was the result of refusing to try something new, something that might get me unstuck. My goal is for you to experience many of the same benefits I did and become a more balanced, mindful, and purposeful being in the workplace. If you can realize those benefits, you will feel pride, optimism, and confidence in the work you do. You can look forward to going to work, to reigniting any lost passion, and instilling a newfound sense of hope and excitement for what's to come. For anyone who feels that's missing in your life, this book can help shift your viewpoint and place you back on a career path where you feel valued and able to achieve your goals.

Chapter 1

You Don't Know What You Don't Know

When I finished my master's degree, I was ready to hit the job market. I had been in college for 6 years. I could not wait to have a real job and checking account balance above $100. Except while I was in college, the economy had started to suffer and by the time I graduated, we were in a full recession. There were no jobs. I joined a local chapter of a professional business association and started networking with its members to try and get my foot in the door somewhere. I applied to over 50 different job postings online. I updated my resume so the language I used under skillsets and experience matched key words listed in the job description. I went up and down streets, walked into every business along the way, and asked if they were hiring. I got the same answer each time. Either I was overqualified because I had a master's degree, or I was underqualified because I didn't have enough work experience. I finally went to multiple temporary agencies and passed along my resume. A few weeks later, I got a call from one of those temp agencies. I was given a 3-month assignment to enter data into a new software system for a mid-sized non-profit.

It was not my dream job. It really wasn't even a job, just a temporary assignment. My dream job was to become a management consultant. That was what I studied when I was in graduate school. It was the job that would allow me to advise and guide many people, and put me in a position where I could serve as a pseudo psychologist across an organization – helping people to find easier and better ways of working. I knew I needed several years of work experience on my resume before making the leap to my dream job. Luckily, the temporary role turned into a permanent position. As I entered data, I found errors that

I had to investigate. I cleaned them up. That led to defining new processes and educating people on policies, protocols, and how to use the new software system, which, in turn, led to a full-time job as the supervisor over the Behavioral Health Department. I began to build out the department. I found new sources of revenue, set up an internship program, and provided regular business process and protocol trainings to therapists and support staff. I was successful by accident, meaning I managed to navigate my way through it. Years later, I realized I unnecessarily took a long and difficult path to get there. I found myself doing a lot of re-work. I was not building a good reputation because it was hard for me to hide my frustration and I often snapped at others in meetings or when they requested more of me. I didn't speak the language. I didn't know there was supposed to be a common language we all spoke. I often did not have the tools or knowledge of the methodology I was using. I would implement a new credentialing process or billing system without knowing someone, somewhere, had already defined the methodology for how to do that successfully.

I was just making it up as I went. I re-invented the wheel. It meant I worked long hours. I was in the office every Saturday. I took my work home with me during the week and was on the phone with colleagues after hours. A few years later, I was burned out. I had worked myself into exhaustion and was ready for a big change. I wanted to move to a new city. I needed a new job.

That was how I got the courage to attempt the leap to my dream job. I was interviewing for my first role as a management consultant. It was something I didn't think I could possibly attain until late in my career. I thought I needed a minimum of 10 years of work experience. However, there I was, 4 years into my career, a naive 20-something, interviewing for the role. I was excited. I was ready.

I trained for this when I got my Master of Organization Development. I spent 2 years in a graduate program focused on helping me become a consultant. I gave presentations to alumni who served as executives for a wide range of companies. They critiqued me, explained how the consulting business worked, and offered up advice. I completed two internships where I played the role of business consultant. I read countless articles, wrote papers outlining how organizations worked, and studied business analogies and trends. I took several workstyle assessments, had classmates fill out anonymous feedback surveys regarding my strengths and improvement areas, and participated in several mock interviews. I immersed myself in the study of how to be an effective consultant. I was so ready for this job.

I can do this; no problem was what I repeated in my head over and over. Fake it until you make it was my motto. I needed to at least appear confident, so I gave myself pep talks. I would think about all the work and training I had done to get this role and how others didn't have that same advantage. I got the interview through a friend, Jill, from my graduate class. She was living in Seattle, the city I wanted to move to, and I had called her up. She said her consulting firm was hiring, asked for my resume, and recommended me to her supervisor for an interview. It was almost too easy. Just like that, the stars had aligned for me. I felt amazing after each interview round, like I knocked it out of the park. I understood how to solve the example business problems the interviewers discussed with me. I told Jill that I knew this was the job for me. And after the third interview round, I got the job offer.

I called Jill to tell her the news. I was elated and told her how I was ready for anything. I gave her my opinion on how to be a good consultant and my plan to tackle any problem thrown my way. In a very matter-of-fact tone, she said, "Well, you've never been a consultant, so you just need to see what it's like. I mean, you don't know what you don't know." I was flabbergasted. Her words felt like an insult. I could not believe she chose to say that versus revel in the excitement with me. After all, we were going to be living in the same city and working together. At that time, I didn't realize *you don't know what you don't know* was a famous quote from Socrates that I would hear regularly from my mentors and managers at the new job. My bigger concern in that moment was that she didn't realize I knew a lot.

Of course I know what I'm doing, I thought. Jill was in my master's program, in the exact same cohort. She sat right next to me in every class. *Why would she think this?* I thought. *And why would she say that to me?* I didn't tell Jill what I was thinking. I just said, "Yeah, true." I didn't want to upset her or have any tension between us. I mean, she had recommended me for the position and was going to be my co-worker. She also was someone I respected and looked up to in graduate school. She was only 5 years older than me, but it made a big difference in terms of work experience, and I felt like she always grasped content in a different and better way than I did.

I vacillated a lot between proving that I knew a lot in the early stages of my new job and keeping my mouth shut to learn what I didn't realize I didn't know. Ultimately, I decided to spend at least a couple months observing to see which was the better route. That meant I had to be open to the idea that maybe there was a lot I didn't know. On my first day at my new job, I kept my mouth shut. I did not share any ideas or opinions because I kept thinking about Jill's response when I did get excited and over-shared. "You don't know what you don't know" rang through my head. In retrospect, keeping my mouth shut and letting those who had been consultants for a long time (or even a year) do the talking was one of the smartest moves I ever made in my entire career.

The first day was spent in new employee orientation, which included the usual boring administrative paperwork for benefits and taxes. However, it also served as a review of key information about what my company did and how, expectations for new employees, and consulting tips and tricks for success. Because I had been knocked off my pedestal and gone from "I have been trained for two years and am ready to conquer this role" to "you don't know what you don't know," I was able to focus on what everyone else said and really take it in. I was the only new hire who took notes that day. I normally would not have, but since I accepted that I had a lot to learn, I brought a spiral notebook with me. There were seven other people in my class. It was clear I was the most focused throughout orientation as I jotted down key points and asked follow-up questions. I felt a little embarrassed, like I may be branded with the undesirable title of new class nerd or suck-up. But I also knew when we walked out of that room that I had absorbed more than most, if not all, of them. What I didn't know was how well this new outlook would serve me.

After new employee orientation, my new hire class was ready to be placed on a project. As management consultants, we got "staffed" on projects with our company's clients. My consulting firm had clients ranging from some of the largest, most influential, and cutting-edge companies in the world to more moderate mid-sized US-based firms. The companies we worked for typically employed between 5000 and 35,000 people. When one of our client companies had a new initiative that needed extra headcount to help launch and implement, they would reach out to our firm to see who was available with the skillset they were looking for. On our end, my consulting firm grouped us into teams based on skillset. That helped everyone quickly identify which type of consulting each of us offered and helped us get staffed quicker.

I was on the Organization Effectiveness team. It aligned to my educational background and skillset. It meant I could help a client with project management, change management, organization design, and Human Resources (HR) related work. While waiting to be staffed, I was informed that new hires were assigned a "buddy" to help them learn how things worked. I was also told I would be assigned an "advisor" to coach me and help get me staffed on my first project. As it turned out, it took about a month to get staffed, and I was on my own because my advisor was out of the office traveling internationally. Luckily, Jill was assigned to be my buddy because of our history together.

I was anxious to start my first project. I felt I had something to prove. I wanted my consulting firm to know they didn't make a mistake hiring me. I wanted to be a valuable employee, a top performer. I was ready to build a name for myself. I felt like a bull in a rodeo, waiting to be let out of my cage so I could show everyone what I was made of. But Jill's words made me think I needed to hit the brakes. When she and I had our first meeting as new hire buddies, I asked her how I should use my time while I waited to be staffed. Building off her advice of "you don't know what you don't know," she essentially told me I needed to know more, and the best way to do that was to learn from people who already had the knowledge. I needed to schedule 30-minute "meet and greets," as she called them. She told me to go to the company directory, look up everyone who was on the Organization Effectiveness team and email them. I was to ask if I could come to wherever they were staffed and have coffee, lunch, or just an afternoon chat to meet them and learn more about their experiences as consultants.

I wasn't thrilled with the thought of reaching out to 20 or so strangers and driving all over a city I was not familiar with for a 30-minute conversation that had the potential to be incredibly awkward. I panicked about what I would say or if they would immediately think I was annoying and requesting too much of their time. I thought their reaction would be "this is dead last on my priority list" or "who is this random person," and I would just be embarrassing myself. However, I quieted those thoughts and followed Jill's advice anyway. After all, she had been doing this for a few years, so she knew better than I did. I was surprised to find that while a few people did not respond, most did, and about half of them had time to meet with me.

I got way more out of those meet and greets than I expected. Since I was meeting people where they were staffed, and they were spread out across multiple companies, one completely unexpected benefit was exposure to a wide variety of work environments. Some of the clients' norm was to dress in jeans and t-shirts, while others looked more like they were attending a black-tie affair. Some were in huge skyscrapers in the middle of a bustling city with restaurants and entertainment venues surrounding us. Others had entire campuses, similar to a university, with endless amenities for their employees, while still others had a quiet little office space they rented out, as most of their employees traveled or worked remotely. Just the revelation that company cultures differed tremendously and that I would need to transform myself to fit in with each, depending on where I was staffed, was a phenomenal learning experience.

As I met with each of my teammates, I remembered my new mantra as the new hire, "you don't know what you don't know" – and I asked questions accordingly. I had three. First, I wanted to hear about their role and typical projects they worked on. Second, I wanted to hear what they had learned, any tips and tricks they could share. Finally, I asked them for any advice they had for a newbie. I initially was concerned that these questions would not be enough to fill our time, but the opposite happened. They had so much to say, we often went over our time. I was captivated with the lessons and advice they provided – like the importance of defining your role expectation upfront, being proactive by researching building names and parking ahead of your first day, the importance of recognizing, and conforming to, the company culture, and the value in being someone who can pivot and flex to meet customer and stakeholder demands. I was in a head space where I was thinking, *I've never been a consultant, so I don't know anything*, which meant I had nothing to say. My sole purpose was to listen and learn. Since that was my only purpose, I did a much better job of hearing and remembering what others had to say.

Another unexpected benefit was everyone appreciated that I took the time to learn from them. I unintentionally made a great first impression because I wanted to learn from those who had been doing what I wanted to do. They lit up when I asked for their advice. It was like they had been waiting for someone to ask, and finally I had come along. Even better, as time went on, these people checked in on me. They became mentors and friends and they wanted to know how I was doing. All of this because I recognized that in my new role, I didn't know anything. I did have work experience and a 2-year program that trained me, but I had not been a consultant. Whether it was my first job or my fifth did not matter. It was a new role, and the best thing I could do was recognize that and learn from those who had been in the role.

What I realized during my conversation with Jill and that first month at my new job was that studying an industry or organizational function was completely and totally different than practicing in one. While I understood larger concepts and knew what the latest trends and research said about several problems that plague an organization, I had not actually ever attempted to fix those issues. Fixing them was different than reading about them. Jill told me it would take 18 months to figure out what was going on. She nailed that timeline. There was so much to learn. For starters, I had to learn all the language they spoke. Each client company spoke in acronyms and different dialects of the same business language. By joining these different companies, I learned it was important to have a language. Describing what needed to be done and how was more efficient and effective if there was terminology provided to the people doing the work. Putting terminology around process steps, methodology, training, and meeting requirements to launch or implement a new initiative aligned everyone to what needed to be done and how. For example, if every new initiative the company rolled out had to call their first meeting a "kick-off," it meant that people would ask when someone was going to "kick-off" the work. It meant that when attendees received a meeting invite with the words "kick-off" in the title, they knew an initiative was being launched, and it would somehow impact them. They came to the meeting ready to listen and learn. This one term aligned everyone and gave us a way to communicate better.

My consulting firm also had a language I needed to learn. Management consultants, as it turned out, have their own expansive vocabulary. I had to learn a lot of terms quickly and change or refine the definition of some that were already in my repertoire. That alone was complex and time consuming, not to mention everything else I needed to understand to be fully onboarded – how to identify and manage risks, how to hold teams accountable to timelines, how to influence people, and really, how to be a good consultant.

Over the next decade, I noticed several times in my career that people wanted to be known as experts within a month of starting a new role. They did not understand the concept of "you don't know what you don't know" and pushed hard to appear fully onboarded. They deemed themselves the go-to person in meetings, but they were not. They merely presented themselves that way. These people failed and became known as overly confident or full of inaccurate information. They were actively avoided by others seeking knowledge and seen as an obstacle by those who worked with them. Thinking that someone can be proficient in a high-level role so quickly was not realistic, and it did not serve anyone in the long-term. People who did well in their roles recognized the time it took to become an expert, valued their team members, and allowed themselves time to learn.

If you think about it long enough, you can apply this to everything in life. Most people understand, for example, that a single 25-year-old with no children giving unsolicited parenting advice to a 45-year-old parent of four is absurd and may even be considered offensive. But stop and think about why. *Why* is that offensive? Because the 25-year-old has not done or experienced what the 45-year-old has. A person cannot truly comprehend something until they have done it themselves. How could someone who is perfectly healthy give a cancer patient advice on how to handle a diagnosis? They can't. Because you don't know what you don't know, and it's ignorant for someone to think they know because they read a few articles, watched a documentary, or knew a couple of patients. It just isn't the same.

This applies just as strongly to the business world. No one wants you to tell them how to do something or even hear your opinion on something you've never done or experienced. Recognize what you don't know and own that you don't know it. It will go much further than pretending or assuming you know about something you have never done. Give yourself the time and space to learn and build your experiences. Learn and master one thing at a time, then move on to the next.

Chapter Summary

Lesson	How to Implement	When to Implement
You Don't Know What You Don't Know	• Internal recognition that you are new and therefore know less than everyone else • Listen intently and take notes • Schedule meet and greets • Ask experienced people for advice • Spend time focused on learning how to speak the language • Be patient with yourself • Know the timeline to fully onboard (or grasp every detail of) your new role (6-24 months to learn a new role, varies based on role level and complexity)	• First job • New job • New company • When a role or initiative you own requires different or additional skillsets than your previous role

Chapter 2

Find the Learning in Everything You Do

When I started my new career, there was much to learn. Since I was using the mantra "you don't know what you don't know," my initial days and months were quite easily filled with learning opportunities. I didn't have to look for them because they were always there. As I progressed through my career, I became one of the experienced people. I found that I quickly became someone whom other people, especially those who were brand new, came to for information or guidance. There were even times when I was the only one on my team who knew how to do something.

As I settled into my role, the development and learning I was experiencing became harder to find. I realized that once the initial learning was complete, it became harder to be intrigued by work. I was regularly assigned new tasks because I was fully onboarded and expected to complete what was thrown my way. There were times I viewed assigned tasks as meaningless, felt frustrated by a request, or even found myself at odds with other colleagues who I felt passed the grunt work along to me. There were also times when I disagreed with the direction a project was going or was responsible for a task I didn't know how to do. It can be hard to find the motivation to push forward in those moments. Like everything in life, we have all experienced ebbs and flows at work. Through managing and coaching others, I've learned that for many people, they feel hopeless when these types of things happen repeatedly. It seems like there's no way out except to quit. While I can relate, I was able to stop feeling that way because I learned about a new perspective that proved there were other ways to view, interpret, and respond to those situations.

On my first consulting project, I was assigned a manager named Stanley. We worked well together, and he eventually became my most valuable mentor. One day he told me about an interaction he had with a group of senior leaders in our company. He was asked to present financial information and progress for one of our client's accounts that he oversaw. He said the reaction he received was frustration. Leadership told him he misinterpreted the request, and the information he captured was not what they needed. They dismissed him from the room. They did not provide him with any immediate feedback about how to improve.

Obviously, that altercation was disappointing and had upset him. I remember being shocked when he told me the story. Stanley was well known as one of our best consultants and had been with the company for close to 10 years. I could not comprehend why, with his reputation and tenure, leadership would not provide more information. I instantly came to his defense and started to critique the senior leaders. He interrupted me and said, "That's not what matters. I need to find the learning in this. I just can't figure out what I'm supposed to learn from it."

I realized his struggle was not what I assumed. If I were in Stanley's position, I would have been focused on how leadership could have improved. Why didn't they elaborate on what information was missing? Why hadn't they given a better explanation of their expectation? I would have been angry if, after putting significant time and effort in, any meeting went that way, but *especially* one with leadership.

Stanley was not angry. His emotional response was more of a frustrated confusion. He was not upset about leadership's unclear direction or perplexing response. The questions running through my head were not the same ones running through his head. He was frustrated because he knew it was an opportunity to better himself and could not figure out what the lesson was.

I stopped talking because I realized that for Stanley, it was not about what happened. It was not about critiquing leadership and pointing out what they could have done better. He did not want or need to rationalize or condemn any wrongdoing on their part. What happened could not be changed. Dwelling on leadership's role would not improve Stanley's ability to do better next time. Stanley knew he was being presented with a learning moment that he did not want to overlook or misinterpret. That day, my respect for Stanley grew significantly. Through that conversation with him, I learned that if I chose to grow and evolve in those moments, even when I could easily point out how others could have better handled the situation, it would be a testament to my character.

After that conversation, I began to observe how others in similar predicaments responded. I started to pay attention when colleagues, stakeholders, and clients were presented with a circumstance where they could choose to focus on how others could improve or how they could. If they responded by pointing the finger outward, I kept a subtle distance from them. They were not the type of people I wanted to learn from. If they chose to rise above their circumstances, find the learning in it, and better themselves because of what they had been through, then I aligned myself with them. I deeply respected them.

For my part, I tried to imitate Stanley's response when I found myself in a comparable situation. The hardest part was mentally removing myself from the anger in moments where I felt less responsible than the other party for the unfavorable business situation we were in. It was hard to turn my attention and focus on the learning. The first time I tried, I kept it together in front of my co-workers but went straight to the gym and worked out hard. I took an exercise ball and slammed it on the floor over and over again until I released the anger. The next time it happened, I felt less irritated. I was able to walk it off and pivot my attention from the unwanted circumstance to the lesson much quicker. Each time it happened, it got a little easier until I no longer felt anger or frustration. I just went straight to a place within myself where I asked what I needed to learn from that experience. The benefit I gained was that I was no longer impacted by what others said, felt, or did. I noticed who did what and why, but instead of reacting, I put distance and boundaries between myself and that person. I then chose to put my effort and attention toward what I could learn to stop it from happening again. Since I consciously made the decision to focus my brain on what I could learn and not over-analyze the role other people played in the story, what they did mattered much less to me. The more I tried to look for the learning, the less others' opinions and behaviors affected me. What mattered was not who to place blame on, but how much I was going to grow because of the situation.

Sometimes, like in Stanley's case, finding the learning in something was hard because the lesson was unclear or the way it was presented was frustrating. Other times, it was because something seemed trivial or boring. My conversation with Stanley was actually the second time someone explained to me that finding the learning in everything was so important. The first time I heard the advice occurred when I was assigned a task that I viewed as below my skillset and a waste of my time and abilities. It happened while I was waiting to be staffed on a project. I was contacted by a staffing coordinator who told me that I would spend a few days helping a vice president at my consulting firm with a presentation. I felt excited and proud. There were several people waiting for a project assignment, yet I was the person the vice president chose to help her with a presentation. I wanted to do a good job because it was my first exposure to senior leadership. I had visions of co-presenting some type of confidential, significant data to key leaders across the company. I was excited to meet with her and learn from her.

The next day, I approached the vice president and asked

how I could help. She smiled and asked if I could create **one** PowerPoint slide over the next couple of days. I thought, *she cannot be serious,* but I said, "Of course." She gave me a document with information the slide needed to summarize and sent me on my way. As I walked out of her office, all I could think was that she did not understand how to use my skillset and abilities. I felt she treated me like her puppy who was excited to see her. She petted me, laughed, and pushed me out the door. I spent a solid hour mulling over how ridiculous her request was. I was in awe of the realization that my dream job could be so boring. Several thoughts crossed my mind over that hour. *Is this normal or does she just think I'm that bad? Is the vice president not very smart about how to use her resources effectively? Is she the type of person who thinks she's better than everyone else?* I mentioned the experience to a colleague to feel out her reaction. She replied, "Just find the learning in it. Find the learning in everything you do."

Learning? In making one slide that she already provided an outline for? I thought. Against my natural reaction and tendencies, I listened to her and asked myself, "How can I learn from this?" From there, I visited our company intranet and searched for examples of presentations vice presidents had given in the past. I emailed a few co-workers and asked for examples of the best slides they had seen. Once I started reviewing the content I had gathered, my mind was blown. These examples were incredible. I never would have thought to create anything like the examples that were provided. They told an entire story through images. I immediately understood the message the slide was trying to convey, even without any context or background. It was astonishing. I realized that if I had not listened to my colleague, I would have given the vice president a ridiculous slide with five bullet points summarizing the outline she shared. I would have handed that to her, not knowing the bar was so much higher.

That day, I was not planning on learning anything. I was

content with sulking about how boring my job was, how awful this vice president was, and how misunderstood my skillset was. Instead, I learned several things. First, I learned that one slide can tell an entire story through pictures and land a message or idea that could easily take 15 paragraphs to explain. Next, I learned that incredible awareness and self-development can come from tasks that initially appear boring and mundane. Most importantly, I learned I needed to be more open-minded. I opened myself up to the possibility that learning could be found in everything I did because of that interaction. The question was whether I would be willing to look for it.

Through these experiences, I realized the importance of the perspective that a person chooses to take at work. I met a lot of people down the road who were offended by the requests they received to do something they considered trivial or below them. That was once my perspective, so it was familiar to me. I had learned that it was the wrong perspective. After making that slide, when I got requests to do something that I considered below my skillset, I asked myself, "What and how can I learn?" When I approached my work from that angle, there was rarely a dull moment. I also never became the person who could use a good dose of humility, a trait I unfortunately found was a lot more common among colleagues than I preferred. I knew there truly was learning in everything I did. I just had to look past feelings of entitlement to see it.

I started my consulting career by actively seeking knowledge. As I began to build my knowledge base, I was reminded of the importance of ensuring I understood something before reacting. That was the action I needed to take to find learning in everything I did. As outlined in the book *The 7 Habits of Highly Effective People*, one must first seek to understand. The author, Stephen Covey, discusses the importance of first seeking to understand, and then being understood. The idea is that in order to perform effectively in a workplace setting, it is imperative to understand others' perspectives and reasoning behind their viewpoint[1]. While Covey primarily focused on how to apply this habit to interactions with colleagues and supervisors, I found it to be a great mantra for all aspects of the workplace. I needed to understand not just people, but also interactions, connections, problems, solutions. I wanted to learn everything.

In terms of people, I always tried to understand a person before responding to them. Many times, I realized that my initial response was off-base because I misinterpreted the intention. When I found myself thinking poorly of a colleague or manager because I did not understand them or assumed their intention, "seek to understand" became my mantra. By taking the extra time to clarify someone's intention before I jumped to a conclusion or reacted based off an assumption, I learned a lot about people – how they operate, what motivates them, and most importantly, how to better communicate with them.

When I was in graduate school, I had a professor tell me, "90 percent of the problems that occur in an organization can be traced back to a miscommunication." That statistic stuck with me throughout my career as I realized how important it was to be clear in my messaging and ensure that I understood what others were communicating. I found that in order to do this, I had to be fluent in multiple languages. Everyone spoke their own language, so to truly understand what others were trying to communicate, I had to learn their language. When I thought about all the different roles in an organization, I realized how many languages and variations of the same language there were. There were engineers, project managers, human resource professionals, business operations managers, accountants, property and facilities managers, information and technology support, quality assurance managers, customer service representatives, sales managers, and the list goes on. Each group spoke their own vernacular of the overarching company language.

Furthermore, sub-groups within those macro-groups each spoke a different dialect of the same language. When I was interacting with these groups, especially for the first time, I had to ask a lot of questions about their language. I clarified terminology and asked what acronyms stood for in one-on-one and small group settings. These questions initially seemed basic, and I was slightly concerned the person I was asking would get irritated, but they were necessary for me to avoid miscommunication. As it turned out, many times the person I was asking was not sure what an acronym meant, nor the full definition of a term used. They were just repeating what others had previously stated. The questions I asked to clarify the terminology each team used ended up helping multiple people because we realized we were playing telephone, and no one stopped to decrypt the message. In those moments, we saved ourselves a lot of time and effort. By clarifying others' messages, I became aware of my own language and began to proactively clarify any term I used that had the potential to be misinterpreted by my audience, particularly in meetings where I collaborated across multiple groups. It took some effort upfront but saved me re-work down the line. My professor had also pointed out that confirming what others' say by paraphrasing and summarizing would ensure I avoided 90 percent of potential risks because I had removed 90 percent of the problems that traced back to a miscommunication. It was much better to proactively solve problems when beginning the work versus being surprised by them toward the end. I had to *seek to understand* all the different languages and dialects with a goal of becoming fluent in each. It was a skillset that differentiated me, added tremendous value to the client firm I was working for, and taught me quite a bit along the way.

As part of my mission to acquire more knowledge, I asked those who I admired to tell me the best piece of advice they ever received in their careers. One colleague told me the best advice she received was, "The harder it hurts, the more you're learning. It's called growing pains." The thought of experiencing growing pains in a work setting had never crossed my mind. I appreciated the type of advice that made the intangible tangible. It was easier to apply. This advice took me to a time and place when I felt I was in a slump. It reminded me of when I had a bad attitude about something. It reminded me of times I was asked to do something I had never done before and did not want to. I felt and knew the pain she was talking about. Sometimes work would literally hurt my brain or make me feel physically overwhelmed. My automatic response when I felt that pain was to vent about how awful my job was. But after I contemplated that advice and decided to adhere to it, I changed my response. In those moments I trained myself to think, *this is painful, so I must be growing*. Then, I sought out the lesson presented and the knowledge I needed to acquire.

It's important to note that growing pains from learning and stretching myself at work are different than pain felt by working too much or truly being mistreated in the workplace. When I received the advice, this was the caveat: I needed to be able to recognize the difference. The way to recognize the difference was to repeat what happened based on the facts. That meant not filling in a storyline based on what I perceived others were thinking, why they were behaving a certain way, or whether or not there was a certain tone or body language that I did not like. That meant I had to stick to only exactly what was said and asked of me. For example, if I worked a 60-hour work week, I had to think about what exactly was asked of me versus where I made assumptions. Did I work 60 hours because I was told to do everything, or did I volunteer to do some of the work? Had I been assigned a due date, or did I offer one up that turned out to be unrealistic? Had I taken the most efficient approach, or did I complete some activities and tasks that could have been a lower priority or skipped altogether?

That was the only way to differentiate whether the challenge I was facing simply required an open mind and growth, or if I was truly being mistreated and working in a toxic environment. If your decisions about how to move past a hurdle or frustration at work are based on the storyline and narrative you create for yourself, then you unnecessarily make yourself the victim and miss out on a learning opportunity.

I felt growing pains when I was pushed out of my comfort zone or asked to do more, but I knew if I made myself do it, my skillset would improve. That meant the next time I was in a similar circumstance, it would not hurt as much because I had already acquired the knowledge to navigate my way through whatever it was that made me feel overwhelmed. Another motivation to push myself to learn was the idea that the same problems continue to present themselves until we acknowledge and address them. One quote that I found particularly helpful came from renowned author and teacher Pema Chodron, who said, "Nothing ever goes away until it teaches us what we need to know." This train of thought was so motivating for me because I realized that if I ignored the lesson presented, it would show up again. There was no way to run or hide from it. If I quit my job without finding the learning in the pain I was feeling, I would be doomed at the next job because the lesson would inevitably repeat itself and find its way into my work-life path until I mastered it.

One of the more popular phrases I learned in the consulting industry was, "Build your toolkit." It meant I needed to build or gather examples of templates and knowledge throughout my career. For example, the first time I managed a new initiative or plan, I needed something to capture tasks, timelines, owners, and dependencies. In my world, it was referred to as a project plan. I built the first one in Microsoft Excel and then saved it and added it to my toolkit. Anytime I needed to build a project plan, I took that template out and leveraged it instead of starting from scratch. With each initiative I worked on, I searched for cool examples of templates and tools and saved them, slowly but surely building my toolkit. While saving templates and repurposing them for each project was a great way to save time, the invaluable part of my toolkit was the intangible lessons I added. My intangible toolkit was made up of knowledge and advice. I referenced it and used the tools regularly when faced with varying problems. I found the learning in what I needed to do in each scenario, and I remembered my lessons. Then, I referenced them when applicable to a new problem I was facing. As I built my toolkit, I became more and more knowledgeable. Then I became more confident and, finally, more comfortable navigating ambiguity on a regular basis. It became normal for me to always be doing something I had never tried before.

To be successful in the business world, I had to change my mindset and approach when I found myself stuck in the trenches or felt overwhelmed by the job. When I was stressed, the first step to moving past it was acknowledgment. I recognized that work was harder than it had been and then questioned what could be learned from the situation. By viewing setbacks as an opportunity to learn, I ended up impressing not only those around me, but more importantly, myself. If I approached each workday by saying, "What can I learn today?" the work became stimulating. That approach enabled me to feel accomplished and proud of my work. I found that when I no longer had anything left to learn, that was the key indicator it was time to walk away from a job.

Whether the problem is big or small, approach it from a standpoint of learning and you will not be disappointed by the results. Learning is in everything we do, and it is something we can draw great achievement from. Regardless of your specific situation, there is something you can learn. Take every moment that has frustrated you and think, *what did I learn?* Then take the lessons you identify, add them to your toolkit, and apply them to new scenarios, people, initiatives, deliverables, and interactions. That's how you build a foundation of knowledge and how you become well-versed in navigating the unknown while staying motivated and positive. Aim first to understand the circumstance and learn from it, and when you feel growing pains from that learning, remember it's temporary – if you push through, you will come out much better on the other side.

Endnote

1. Covey, Stephen R. *The 7 Habits of Highly Effective People: Powerful Lessons in Personal Change.* Fireside, 1989.

Chapter Summary

Lesson	How to Implement	When to Implement
Find the Learning in Everything You Do	• Focus on what lesson is being presented when difficult situations or menial tasks present themselves • Become fluent in multiple languages • Proactively avoid miscommunication by clarifying terminology, paraphrasing, and summarizing • Recognize growing pains (and that they are different than pain caused from being overworked or mistreated) • Seek to understand • Build your toolkit • Stay humble	• Communicating with people • Understanding people's intentions • Completing requests from leadership or customers • Receiving feedback and/or critique of your work

Chapter 3

Ask Questions That Get to the Solution

As I built knowledge through learning and seeking the advice of others, I moved myself in the direction of becoming a thought leader, someone who solved problems. Thought leadership was a term I first heard colleagues use to describe people they learned from. It was a quality that was evident in the questions people asked, solutions they provided, and conversations they had. One important observation I began to make in an effort to identify thought leaders was what people brought to the table when a problem arose at work. I was surprised to find that most people brought the same thing to the table: the ability to identify a problem and argue different perspectives on what the root cause of it was. That begged the question, how valuable was it for someone to be able to debate the reason a problem occurred?

If I use a simplified analogy about having a problem, like nothing to eat in the refrigerator, it's easy for me to see that debating the problem is a useless way of resolving it. The average person who opens a refrigerator door to discover there is barely any food would solve the problem by going to the grocery store versus researching who ate what and why. They might wonder who ate it and why, but they know that to solve the issue of being hungry, they have to go get more food. Over time, I realized that focusing on the solution, not the problem, was the best approach. There were times when I did need to clearly understand the root cause of the problem in order to solve it, but many times I did not. One of the best ways I demonstrated value in the workplace was to solidify my reputation as someone who was a solution-oriented force within an organization.

During the first few months of my career, Jill played an active role in coaching me. When I was first staffed on a new project, I struggled to follow conversations since I was still learning the language. I had a hard time figuring out what to clarify and how because I couldn't always follow the terminology used to describe a problem. Jill gave me a few pointers on this. First, she said to write down terms I was unfamiliar with and privately follow up with colleagues I trusted to learn the meaning. Second, she told me to focus on the context. That way it would be easier to make an educated guess about the definition, and I would not miss the point as long as I still followed the overall context. Her final piece of advice was not to ask questions unless they clarified the path to the solution. Any other question I had was a waste of time. My purpose was to solve problems, so the questions I asked should correlate to my purpose. Therefore, if a question did not move me closer to a solution, it really did not need to be asked.

I was hesitant when I first heard that advice. All I could think was, *there must be some type of exception to this rule*. I tried to come up with an example of when it made sense and was helpful to ask a question that was not specifically moving us closer to the solution. I was stumped. All I could come up with was that I could ask questions like "How was your weekend?" or "How are your kids doing?" to build rapport with someone before a meeting. However, during a meeting with a supervisor, customer, client, leader, or stakeholder to discuss an initiative I was working on, I realized she was right. There was no point in asking anything that did not clarify how we would make forward progress and arrive at our final goal. This helped me to realize when I was about to ask a question that did not really matter. All I had to say to myself was, "Will this question get me closer to the solution?" before I asked it out loud. A lot of the questions that came to mind initially were details – what if scenarios that were unlikely to happen but could, specific owners of a step within a broader process that wasn't yet fully built, or ideas I had about a related topic but were not the focus of the meeting that day. While some of these things may have been applicable down the road and were somewhat related to the conversation at hand, they did not directly address the problem we aimed to solve in that meeting and therefore did not need to be asked in the moment. After applying this piece of advice to my daily routine, I realized that people started to see me differently. They were quiet and attentive when I spoke because they learned over time that any question I asked would be meaningful and useful. I realized they were beginning to see me as a thought leader.

The complexity of business problems I faced throughout my career varied greatly. While they were typically more complex than what to do about an empty refrigerator, they were also regularly over-complicated. A year into my career, I was staffed on a new project that was above my pay grade. I was informed the person initially assigned was no longer available. Even though that person was a couple levels higher than I was at my company, I agreed to take on the project. I was up for a good challenge and knew it was an opportunity to expedite myself through the learning curve I was on as a new hire. I also saw it as an opportunity to put the knowledge and advice I was acquiring to good use. Plus, Stanley would be my manager, and I knew he would help me navigate my way through.

My first day, the client and I met for 2 hours to go over how I could help him. The primary goal was to expand the firm's online footprint of retail stores globally. The secondary goal was to open a few new brick-and-mortar stores. The client's company had a handful of retail stores throughout the US as well as an online presence across North America. All of the supply chain capabilities were located in the US. They wanted to expand their brick-and-mortar presence to a few countries across Western Europe, Australia, and Asia and their online presence to all countries in those regions. That meant building out a supply chain and distribution channel per country, working with legal and trade teams to advise on local laws, working with product owners on updating items to the localized language per country, and a host of other hurdles. It was a complex problem we needed to solve to say the least.

In order to get the work up and running, we needed to identify our team. The team would be made up of employees from the client firm who were located in each country we wanted to expand into and had the expertise/skillset we needed. We estimated 50 to 100 people, and they would need to dedicate many hours to this initiative in addition to their regular job duties. That meant we had to ensure their leaders were bought into the goal and aligned to our plan. Leadership would need to identify which of their direct reports could serve on the team. They would ensure those picked had the bandwidth to work with us by removing responsibilities so their directs could have time dedicated to our initiative. There were so many dimensions to such a massive initiative that I didn't know where to start. I debriefed Stanley, and he asked me what the problem was we were solving. I repeated everything we needed to do. He said, "No, summarize what the problem is in one to two sentences. It's called a problem statement." I paused and realized I could not articulate a simplified problem statement.

I took the rest of that day to sort through all of the information that had been thrown at me, and it finally came to me. The problem was that we needed to enable supply chain capabilities across the globe in order to offer products to a wider customer base. The next day, I met with the client and shared the problem statement with him. He was enthusiastic about simplifying the problem. He changed it from a "problem statement" to a "business case" and pointed out that this would enable us to avoid any debates about what we were doing and why. In that moment, we were able to align ourselves on the issue and turn our attention toward how to resolve the problem. That was when I learned the importance of simplifying problems. Even a vast and multi-faceted problem like this one could be simplified. I had to get to the root and move on. I summarized the problem, got agreement, and focused on the solution. We needed to make progress as quickly as possible and that meant identifying steps to get to the solution, not wasting time debating the problem. In order to avoid a scenario where others were distracted by the problem, we leveraged the statement by sharing it first with anyone who joined the initiative. That taught the team to accept the problem and focus on how to make forward progress without putting us in a position where we seemed authoritative or forceful about the work we were doing. The approach worked incredibly well. The project and team members were recognized by the executives as making forward progress in record time. Team members were proud to be part of our initiative and appreciated the recognition they received. I learned that simplifying and aligning to the business problem within a day or two was a great way to skip debates about what went wrong or should've been done, and get a group of people to fully focus on what to do about it.

For every initiative I worked on, unexpected problems or issues always arose during the planning and implementation stages. An unforeseen circumstance would present itself, requiring us to change gears and figure out how to resolve the issue before we could move on. These unforeseen issues were most often reviewed and discussed in the context of a meeting. I found that the typical process was for a problem to first be discussed in a smaller setting among two or three people who were primarily responsible for resolving it. If the size or impact of the problem was widespread or important, there would be a follow-up meeting that involved a broader audience of stakeholders. It was in those broader meetings that I was able to observe how others approached and resolved problems. Over time, I realized that the thought leaders, the people whom others admired and listened carefully to, had a primary goal of asking questions that got to the solution.

I was coached by mentors to know my purpose and role in a meeting before attending it. There were times when I was simply a note taker and not meant to take the reins and solve the problem. In those times, I still asked clarifying questions if I thought it would help the group make forward progress, but only spoke if absolutely necessary. I was always careful and thoughtful in planning what I wanted to say before I actually spoke, and it was only when I thought the answer would be of value to the audience. I was taught early on in my career that the goal, no matter what the circumstance, should always be to add the most value possible. Whether I was attending a meeting, having a hallway conversation, reviewing a deliverable, sending an email, or ordering lunch for a meeting, I always came from the angle of *how to add the most value* in each particular circumstance. Since I was passionate about my career, it was easy to see that the more value I added, the better off I would be. If I wanted to be a team member who was respected by others, I needed to be someone who made every situation I was placed in better.

Many people did not seem to grasp the idea of how or when to add value. Throughout my career, I met people who thought the longer their tenure, the more valuable they became. While I agreed that more work experience expanded a person's knowledge base, that did not translate to the amount of value a person added to their team or organization. The ability of a person to collaborate with others and steer a conversation or meeting toward finding the best solution to resolve a problem was what added the most value to an organization.

As I attended more meetings over my career, I noticed another pattern that emerged. People believed the way to be valuable was by making others aware of their presence in meetings. Many would speak up and voice their opinion unprompted. Other attendees would stop and listen, but I could see on their faces they had the same question as me. What was the point the person was trying to make? More importantly, how was it helpful to the conversation? The issue was the person speaking believed that being noticed equaled being valued, so they spoke up but rarely said anything that mattered. Some people, in their quest to be seen and heard, even took the conversation off topic. That technique had the opposite effect than intended. People who wanted to be heard but had nothing to say were not listened to by others. Senior leaders interrupted them or spoke over them because they did not want to waste any more time. Anytime I found myself with the desire to speak, I first thought about if it would add value to the conversation. If not, I chose to listen and learn instead. Speaking up without saying anything of importance was not the way to build a good reputation, and it certainly never helped move the group toward any type of solution. When I was unsure what to say or how to add value, I asked questions that enabled us to make forward progress. For example, if I was in a meeting where a new initiative was discussed, I asked questions that clarified what we were doing, how, and why. It was important for me to genuinely believe that there were no stupid questions. If it helped clarify the path forward, then it could not be stupid. It was possible people already knew the answer, but if I did not, it was also possible at least one other person did not, and that meant it was worth asking. I found that much of the time when I asked what I thought was a simple, basic question, no one knew the answer. Yet, somehow the more complex questions seemed easier for others to answer. There were also times where I did not fully understand a solution someone else was offering up. In moments where I was not sure what question to ask, and I was not fully comprehending what was being shared, I simply said, "Say more." I noticed Jill doing this often in her conversations, so I tried it. The first time I used it with my client, it felt uncomfortable but worked. My client explained the concept in more detail. It helped me gain a better understanding so I could ask the type of questions that moved us toward the solution.

Concentrating on the solution and focusing my questions on information that got me closer to it was the key to communicating effectively in a business setting. The rest was just fluff – extra and unnecessary. The ability to recognize and remove fluff was key to learning how to ask good questions. When colleagues and stakeholders spoke to me about work, they often added unnecessary commentary to their explanations. I had to learn how to sort additional commentary out from what mattered. I first learned the concept of removing fluff through Jill's review of my written communication. I had her read a few of the emails I sent during my first few weeks on a project to see if she had any feedback. Her first question was why I used words like "I think" or "I believe" at the beginning of a sentence. She told me to come out and say what needed to be said. She said, "It's not I think this, it's just this." I did not realize at that time I even included those phrases, but as I reviewed my emails, I saw it was at the beginning of almost every sentence. I viewed it as my opinion and recommendation, but Jill was right – it was much better to say, "We need to review the remaining budget dollars before moving forward" versus "I think we need to review…"

The next portion of fluff I had to learn to remove was any sentence that distracted from my point. Every time I wrote an email, I read each sentence carefully and asked myself if that sentence was necessary for the reader to hear. I often drafted emails or documents that required someone else to review before finalizing or sending. When I initially wrote the email to the reviewer, my instinct was to include details. I thought it was a way to ensure the reviewer had all the information. I thought providing every detail was a way to proactively manage any opportunity for misinterpretation. However, including all of the details actually made it more difficult for my audience to process the request. My intent was good, but my execution was wrong. It was easy for the reader to get caught up in the details, which distracted from my point and increased the potential for confusion. I included sentences that described what the key takeaways should be, or which sections of a document needed a more detailed review, or I explained a paragraph in the document that may be difficult for the reader to interpret. When I read the email from the viewpoint of my intended audience, I asked myself if the extra context was helpful. The answer was almost always no. The point was that I was asking someone to open my attachment, review my document, and make revisions. If there was something in the document that was difficult to interpret, or that could be misconstrued, the reviewer would point it out in their response. I learned to change my email to get to my point. I asked for the attachment to be reviewed by a specific date and thanked the person for their time and effort. I removed anything that could not stand up to the question, "So what?" If there was no point to the sentence, then it was fluff. Differentiating between fluff and the good stuff was a key skillset that enabled me to communicate clearly. It also helped me collaborate better with others.

There was only one piece of advice I received several times from multiple people in my career. It was to bring them my solutions, not my problems. The first time I heard it was a few months into my career, and it seemed to pop up every year or two afterward, always with a new manager or client. Not because I was not doing it. It was a piece of advice they would say when I first met them. It was a way for them to proactively set expectations and ensure I was a solution-oriented team member. I understood because I knew it would make their lives, and my own, so much simpler. I was specifically told by Stanley, "An undergraduate student can identify a problem. A graduate student can identify a solution. Which one are you?"

Unfortunately, I found in my career and over a decade of observing others that most people were undergraduate students. I saw so many people get excited when they identified a problem, not understanding that what they noticed was already a known issue and the real way to add value was to solve it. Worse yet, they immediately shared their findings with others. In every case, the response was "Yes, we know." The fact is, problems are easy to identify, and there are countless opportunities to find something wrong with how things were done. The hard part, where most people got stuck, is identifying the corresponding solution. Furthermore, I learned that many of the problems identified were more complex to solve than they appeared to be – like not having the technology to support a process change. While it may look like we just need to change one step in a process to fix an issue, because the cost and effort behind implementing a new software system isn't possible or not the priority at the moment, it is easier to continue to work around the problem. In this example, it may seem like it would be useful to point out the problem, but in all actuality, the problem has already been identified, discussed, and solved for.

When I think about this concept, a good analogy for me is politics. When I discuss it with family or friends, there is no doubt that the government is a complicated system made up of a lot of rules, laws, and governing bodies that can and do contradict one another. Many people complain about the government, how it works, and what issues plague it. However, it's very rare that anyone focuses their debate on the solution. People can identify problems all day long but never come up with a comprehensive alternative solution. Business settings are similar. There are a lot of policies, teams, and cultural norms we need to work within, and that makes it much more difficult to find the right solution.

I could point out several problems within the first week of any role I ever filled. I would be assigned to a new client firm, walk in knowing little to nothing about their culture, processes, technology, and people, and suddenly notice that there was a problem with the system I was using, a process people were executing, or a report given to me. I noticed these issues but found ways to work around them versus announcing what I thought was being done incorrectly. I knew that if I pointed out everything that was obviously wrong, it could be misconstrued as insulting my client's intelligence. If I could identify a problem within one week with minimal exposure, certainly someone who had been there day-in and day-out for years had discovered these problems as well. Most likely, the people working there had already discovered those problems along with a host of other issues that I was unaware of. As businesses grew and changed, more problems surfaced and had to be prioritized. Sometimes a problem was not big and impactful – it was just annoying, like manually formatting a report versus having the ability to choose the format and layout when you export it. Some problems were not worth the effort and time to resolve; they just needed to be worked around. That was why I found that sometimes people were content with the issues. Or even if they were not, the problem that had been identified was not the priority and, therefore, not where I needed to spend my time. It was not what my client asked me to focus on and surfacing it or trying to resolve it was not the best way for me to be effective with my time and effort. I learned to stay in my lane. I helped with problems that I was asked to help with. Finding other issues that needed attention was not hard. Focusing on the ones that I was engaged to solve was. That was where I needed to prioritize my time. Many times, a problem I was assigned already had a solution, it just wasn't ideal. If I wanted to truly solve something, I first needed to identify what existing solution was in place. Then, I had to find a better one. Finding a better solution was something to get excited about. That forced me to get creative and push myself to really reflect, contemplate, and innovate. When I learned how to do that, I went from being an undergraduate student to a graduate student.

In order to speak to business problems, I had to learn how to articulate risk. That also meant learning how to mitigate risk. Mitigating a risk means managing or resolving the risk's impact to the business. It was yet another dimension to the solution-oriented skillset I was developing. It was difficult to clearly articulate risk and how it impacted a business when a problem presented itself. Not surprisingly, it was even harder to identify a corresponding mitigation plan. Articulating risk was not the same as stating a general problem; it was more well thought out. A risk had to clearly call out the impact to the business, project, or group, and that was not always inherently clear. For example, if a stakeholder or team member resigned, I knew it was a problem. But the risk could not be "Amy quit." That left room for misinterpretation and did not clarify the impact. The simplest way to get to the meat of the risk was to ask myself why something was a problem three to five times. When someone left a job, the risk was often the person had a key responsibility (or multiple) that only she knew how to do, and others were dependent on. So, in this example I would answer the question, "Why was Amy's departure a risk to the business?" If Amy worked in payroll, it could be because no one else was trained on the payroll system. However, even though that statement provided more context about the problem, it was a vague explanation, so I had to ask myself why again. The second why might lead me to a clearer answer, like Amy was the only person who was given system permissions to approve employee paychecks to be automatically deposited. While asking why for the second time sometimes got me to the heart of the risk, other times, like in this case, the magnitude and timing of the impact remained unclear.

Each time I asked myself why something was a risk, it required me to dig deeper. That sometimes meant I had to talk to other people and gather more information. In this example, I would have to learn from the payroll team and information technology (IT) about how to add another approver to the system and train him or her. By the fifth "why," I typically had a clear risk that did not leave room for interpretation, such as, "Due to a vacancy in the payroll administrator role, no one has access to approve automated deposits for next week's payroll." Risks must be articulated in a way that a random person with no context or background can read and understand it without question. Clear and concise is always the objective.

The goal is the same when identifying a mitigation plan. With mitigation plans, I found there were often a few options that needed to be investigated by considering factors such as cost, effort, and time. To build off the above example, Amy could assign approver rights and train someone before she left, or possibly IT could provide someone from payroll with approver access. I would have to consider if that person could train himself or if tutorials were available. I also would have to consider if this could all be done before the next payroll cycle. Even within my simplified example, multiple options would need to be investigated. There were also multiple steps to each mitigation plan. In this example, before training someone, the first step would be to identify an approver. In addition, I would need to identify who should be trained and likely recommend two or three people be cross-trained. Keeping up with the goal of ensuring mitigations are clear and concise, I would read my mitigation plan and ask myself the same question as when I documented the risk. Could someone with no background or context understand this? In addition, I had to ask myself if the mitigation plan clearly and comprehensively resolved the risk. If it did not, I added information to address each aspect of the risk. I never presented risks without an associated mitigation plan. While time consuming and difficult, identifying and articulating risks and mitigations got easier with practice. Over time, I began to document risks and mitigation plans quickly and easily. This skillset was key to solidifying my ability to be solution-oriented.

Positioning yourself as a thought leader allows you to have greater influence and impact on an organization, which means you can add more value on a larger scale. Thought leaders are focused and driven in their discussions and ability to break apart and resolve a problem. Don't waste your time trying to think of a question or commentary that you believe could be a smart, witty, or insightful addition to the conversation. Focus your energy on identifying ways to make forward progress by asking questions that get closer to the solution. Only speak to add value to a discussion and remove fluff from your conversations. Put in the effort it takes to know how to identify a business risk and mitigation plan. It will serve you well in the long-term. Know when a problem needs to be understood and when it does not. Most importantly, never call out a persistent problem unless you have spent time thinking about how it could be improved. By training yourself to be solution-oriented, you'll find that you stand out among the crowd. Your presence will be known and felt without you needing to say a word.

Chapter Summary

Lesson	How to Implement	When to Implement
Ask Questions that Get to the Solution	• Ask yourself if the question you have will get you closer to the solution before asking it • Simplify a business problem by condensing it into a 1-2 sentence statement • Come from a place where your goal is always to add value • Use the phrase "say more" if you're unsure what to ask • Remove the fluff from your communication • Be a graduate student • Document risks and mitigation plans in a clear and concise manner • Ask yourself "why" three to five times to ensure a risk is clear • Ask yourself if your mitigation plan comprehensively solves all aspects of the risk	• Overcoming a hurdle or obstacle in the workplace • Discussing problems in the context of a meeting • Launching or managing a new project or initiative • Completing requests from leadership or customers • Documenting risks/issues and mitigation plans

Chapter 4

Be Buttoned Up

The highest learning in my career occurred by asking the right people the right questions. The question that yielded the greatest insight was, "What's the best piece of advice you ever received?" I only asked those I respected and admired. "Always be buttoned up" was Jill's response. When I first heard it, I paused for a minute to try and process what it meant. I thought I grasped the general concept, that you must be professional in how you share information, but felt I was missing the deeper meaning. I asked her to elaborate. I told her I was not quite sure how to interpret that advice. She replied, "You'll figure it out." While I didn't appreciate her response in that moment, I did figure it out. There was deeper meaning behind it and several dimensions to remaining buttoned up. The best part was that her advice became the action I needed to take to build a strong reputation, often referred to as a brand, within my firm and across client companies.

The idea that I was a brand, like a type of spaghetti sauce at the grocery store, was referenced several times by multiple people throughout my career. At that time, it was not a well-known concept. Since then, it's been popularized, and is recognized by many, even included as a class topic or part of the curriculum in many business graduate programs. It really hit home for me. I particularly liked the idea of thinking of the reputation I was building as a brand because it removed the personal affiliation for me. If I viewed my reputation as the brand associated with a type of product, then I shifted my way of thinking. The *product* in this case being management consultants, and the *brand* being the unique set of attributes I bring to the table. Through this lens, criticism and feedback became constructive and

48

helpful; there was no need to take something personally if the information was intended to improve the brand of the product I was offering, versus me as a person. I viewed it as data that I gathered to determine how to improve the brand. It forced me to have a better self-awareness and assess myself along my career path in an impersonal, non-damaging way. "What makes my sauce better than the next?" was the question I asked myself. I thought, *if my colleagues and I are all a brand of spaghetti sauce, why would the customer pick me over someone else? What do I really want my brand to be and represent?* By thinking through these questions, I was defining my brand. That was really the first step I needed to take in my quest to build one. I realized part of my brand was what I was good at, my skillset. The other part was how I was viewed by my customers. *Was my brand a trusted and consistent one?* I thought. I wanted it to be. I wanted my reputation to be smart and savvy. I wanted to be known as dependable and well-respected, but I didn't know how to build that type of reputation. As it turned out, the "be buttoned up" advice was what got me there.

Since Jill had not shared the details of what it meant to "always be buttoned up" and cleverly passed the reins to me to ponder, I initially started by remaining professional. I remained professional in my reactions, interactions, and communication. Not surprisingly, emotions were a common thing in the workplace. Even though we were taught there was no place for them, the workforce is human. Emotions are an integral piece of our beings, and therefore impossible to fully break from when a person is spending 40+ hours per week in an office setting. However, keeping this "be buttoned up" mantra in mind was the key that unlocked the mystery of how to separate my emotions from my verbal and non-verbal reactions.

An emotional response to problems, such as working with a difficult person or dealing with unexpected issues, would not help me in my mission for knowledge and solutions. Before I spoke in any work setting, I would tell myself "stay buttoned up," and it allowed me to express myself in a way that didn't reveal what emotion I was feeling. That helped me to ensure no one misinterpreted my responses and comments as personal attacks or critiques on them. My goal to stay buttoned up took away my ability to say what I sometimes felt when a problem arose, like, "Great, now I have to work 50 extra hours to resolve something that should not be my problem." Instead, I would think through the buttoned-up response and simply say, "I'll look into this" because everything else I wanted to say was not professional. Since I always asked myself the question, "Is that response buttoned up?" before I communicated, I stopped myself from reactions and expressions that could be viewed as unprofessional. It took some extra effort initially, but once I was able to consistently and consciously control urges to react with frustration or express my opinion on what others did wrong, I began doing it naturally.

I started to experience the consequences of remaining buttoned up within a couple of months. I noticed my brand was steadily improving and becoming more well known. Since I consistently avoided a reaction or comment that could be interpreted as inappropriate or immature, people saw me as someone who kept it together, did well under pressure, and put thought and effort into my words and approach. I became a trusted advisor to my clients, colleagues, and stakeholders. People I didn't know reached out for advice because someone we had in common told them I was "really good." The funny part was, I was not necessarily better equipped to provide advice, nor was I someone who felt calm and centered in stressful moments. I didn't have some type of secret power or rare skillset others spoke of. In fact, in most cases, there was someone else with a better skillset or more experience who could have given better advice than me. But since that person did not have the right frame of mind, or present themselves in a buttoned-up manner, it didn't matter.

That was the true differentiator between my brand and someone who did not see the value in being buttoned up.

As I continued to apply the buttoned-up rule, I grew less and less attached to my work on a personal level. Staying buttoned up at work, but coming home and being me, made it much easier to check in and out of work every day. It allowed me to stay focused on my personal life at home and easily detach from my workday. It was a new experience for me – to not have my head filled with thoughts about what happened at work that day or what would be waiting for me the following day. It was a newfound freedom that I eagerly welcomed into my life. I started to master checking in and out of work by visualizing a coat hanger in the entryway of my home. When I walked in the door after a long day at work, I paused in the entryway. I pictured myself hanging up my "work coat," the pockets stuffed full of work emails, to do lists, meeting reminders, conversations that exhausted me, and interactions with colleagues. This would signal to my mind that I was removing the burden of work and I needed to fully check out. When I left every morning, I visualized myself putting that work coat back on and mentally checked back in. I learned the ability to check in and out was more about strengthening my brain muscle by learning how to better control my thought patterns. Pausing in the entryway of my home before I left and when I returned everyday was a form of meditation. Physically stopping to stand still and clear my mind for 1 to 2 minutes was a necessary exercise to enable myself to build that brain muscle. It allowed me to fully focus on stopping or restarting thought patterns and processes regarding work. There was my work life and my home life, and the two were very separate for me because at work I was so cognizant of my words and actions that I really enjoyed my personal time when I could let my guard down. The additional benefit was that at work, I was more engrossed and present. My thought processes were clearer and sharper because I had several hours to decompress and unplug every day. That allowed me to think differently and better about problems and solutions when I was checked in. It aided my ability to build that smart and savvy brand I was hoping for.

While the best advice I got came by asking the right people for it, there were also days when a great piece of advice fell into my lap. One day, I was on my lunch break when a colleague asked if she could join me in the cafeteria. We were making small talk when she mentioned she majored in communications in college and that the words of her favorite professor had stuck with her throughout her career. He told her, "It doesn't matter what you say; it only matters what the other person hears." I categorized that advice under the "be buttoned up" umbrella and used it as a guide when reviewing and thinking through my communication with stakeholders. It was a particularly good reminder in written communication. I would review my emails and try to see it from the recipient's perspective before sending. I would ask myself two questions: 1) was my reasoning for reaching out clear? and 2) could what I wrote be misinterpreted as offensive or condescending in any way, shape, or form? I read my email as if I were the recipient and scrutinized it closely. I rewrote sentences that had any possibility of setting the wrong tone.

I had previously been given the advice to "mind my Ps and Qs" when writing an email. I used my manners in everything I wrote and always said please and thank you. I remember overhearing colleagues complain about people being overly sensitive to their emails or being irritated or annoyed when they had to go out of their way to soften an email by saying please or thank you. I never understood why it was stressful to them. It took a few extra seconds and went a long way. The return was worth the investment for me. It seemed like people rarely heard thank you and appreciated it far more than I expected. These tips and tricks on how to interact with others helped me make a positive first impression and added to my ability to remain buttoned up in my interactions. By being overly cognizant of keeping a respectful tone, remaining polite in my delivery, and speaking only to the point I needed to make, I maintained much more control over what the recipient heard and how they responded. While no one can control everything, having more awareness of what I communicated heightened my ability to recall information. In addition, my conversations became shorter and clearer. That made me a more efficient and effective communicator.

Staying buttoned up in conversation forced me to understand the technique of talking about work in an impersonal manner, meaning I learned to talk about the work, not the person. Staying buttoned up became less of an action I took and more of a language I spoke as I further developed the skill. I became very aware of the terminology I used to describe the work that needed to be done. I learned to use terms like action item, deliverable, asks, owner, due date, risk, and mitigation. These terms replaced language that placed blame or focus on an individual person. There were many times in my career where the work I needed to complete was dependent on someone else. I often had to email people who I did not know well and ask them for information. Instead of saying phrases like "I need this" or "you are supposed to provide this," I would say, "I have an ask I'm hoping you can help with." The word "ask" helped me avoid any risk that the receiver of my communication could misconstrue my intent. Many people in the workplace were sensitive to others' asks. They understandably did not want to be assigned more work by anyone who was not their direct supervisor. If the request was not posed in the right way, they assumed they were being talked down to, taken advantage of, or set up to be blamed. I wanted to avoid any scenario where others were offended by my requests or unnecessarily read further into them. When offended or frustrated, people tended to avoid. They would choose not to respond at all to an email, particularly if it required them to do additional work or research.

Requesting something of someone I did not supervise also regularly occurred in a meeting setting. Often it was during meetings that tasks were defined and needed to be assigned. I learned to call tasks we identified "action items" and call the person assigned to each the "owner." By speaking to action items, due dates, and owners, I removed the personal side of the work and overcame my concern that the recipient of the message would feel offended or retaliatory toward me when I discussed progress we needed to make. That was a key aspect to embodying the principle of being buttoned up. I needed the tools and language to be able to exist in that frame of mind. Learning the language helped me bring risks and issues to the forefront without being forced into any sort of conflict with my stakeholders or colleagues. If someone did not complete an action item by the due date, I said, "This action item is past due" in a meeting versus "Mario didn't follow through." I stayed buttoned up by taking my own opinion and personal frustration out of the equation. I only stated facts about the status of the work we were doing, never the person. That was the key to maintaining positive relationships in the workplace. It allowed me to build my brand, even with groups of people who others found impossible to work with.

Another term that served me well was "Subject Matter Expert" or SME. My position required me to coordinate across multiple stakeholders and track and manage their action items. Sometimes the owner of the action item was clear because the task plainly fell within their job responsibilities. Other times, ownership was assigned based on knowledge and experience. When that occurred, people were less likely to accept the task. They didn't see it as part of their job duties, and, therefore, de-prioritized the ask. I would say to them, "Since you are the SME in this situation, we really need to lean on your expertise to get this complete." Recognizing someone as an expert in a specific area, regardless of my own opinion of their skillset, was a helpful way to get his or her agreement to own and complete the assigned action item. It also put a positive tone on the intent, again avoiding the pitfall of offending anyone. It worked best in front of a group of people, such as in a meeting, because I was complimenting that person in front of their colleagues and leadership. I was also gaining that person's commitment in front of everyone to complete an action item. I never used this approach with ill intent, it was simply to recognize why the individual was the best for the job – because they were the expert. Calling that out was both accurate and necessary to increase the likelihood the person would buy-in to helping us. These techniques took time to learn and master. However, just like anything in life, the more effort and practice I put into them, the easier they became. Over time, it was just the way I did things and the way I spoke.

I found that people followed through when I used these techniques. It made my work life much easier because I was often dependent on others to complete their work before I could complete mine. On the rare occasion that someone did not complete an action item they committed to, or never responded to an ask in an email, I followed up. I never took it personally and just followed up two to three times. If there was still no response or follow through, I escalated the situation to that person's supervisor or the person accountable for the overall initiative. I only spoke to what the risk was in terms of the ability to make progress. I never spoke about the person's lack of responsiveness or inability to complete work they committed to. That was for their supervisor to be concerned with, as it was a personnel issue. By remaining buttoned up, I removed any personal stake I felt in someone else completing work. I learned that as long as I raised the risk and continued to focus solely on the work and not the people, it would resolve itself every time. Sometimes the supervisor I escalated to would reach out to the person, who would then complete the ask. Other times, the action item was never completed, but we made progress anyway. We moved around it. I knew that the consequences for the person who did not follow through were not my concern and should not be my focus. My concern was me, the work I was responsible for, the lessons I was learning, and the brand I was building.

Ownership was another key element of staying buttoned up. If I genuinely owned my words, actions, and reactions, it was the best way to ensure I didn't do anything I regretted or had any "I never should have said that" moments. Some people in the workplace seemed to pick and choose which behaviors they owned. It was as if they temporarily developed a convenient form of amnesia when they reacted with anger or frustration toward others. Almost as though it wasn't them who acted or spoke offensively. While that may be their prerogative in their personal lives, in the workplace, everything people do affects their reputation. No one got the luxury of picking and choosing which behaviors they owned. There were no do-overs. We all had no choice but to own all of it. I wanted the things I said and did to be constructive. I wanted to feel accomplished and proud of my work. I didn't want my career to be something I looked back on and felt disappointed about. I already knew that feeling.

I had not built a great brand at my first job. Years later, when I stopped to reflect, I realized that it affected my emotional and mental well-being. It became okay for me to snap and be in a foul mood because I felt I was owed something. I had put in a lot of long hours and hard work, and everyone still expected more. I was offended that others didn't recognize my hard work and I reciprocated by not caring about how I came off to others. I continued to work hard and when I inevitably burned out and had nothing left to give, I was rude to others on a fairly regular basis. I chose not to think about it, and that meant I wasn't owning my behaviors and actions. On the rare occasion that I did stop to think about it, I felt disappointed in who I was becoming. I was allowing my work life to bleed into my personal life, which meant I was in a lousy mood even when I was clocked out for the day. When I started my new job, I consciously controlled myself and my reactions better. When I learned to use the buttoned-up technique, it resolved the issue altogether. I no longer had to put in a huge level of effort to consciously control any tendency to snap at others. I began to truly learn what it meant to own everything I said and did, the bad and the good. It motivated me to keep myself in check. What really surprised me was the pride I felt when my reputation grew more and more stellar. I worked hard to remain centered and focused regardless of what was thrown at me, and it paid off big.

Intend for your brand to be one that works toward solutions and uncovers knowledge in a respectful and gracious manner. Own your actions and thoughts even when you don't want to. Use the phrase "be buttoned up" to get you there. By staying buttoned up in your interactions with others, you will never have to analyze a conversation or concern yourself with what others think. This will allow you to separate your work life from personal and affirm your reputation as a trusted and respected advisor. Most importantly, staying buttoned up will allow you to rightfully earn feelings of accomplishment and pride. People will begin to reach out to you for advice. They will say, "I heard great things about you," or tell you how much they enjoy working with you. Those types of compliments and interactions are bigger and better than being good at your job. They have a deeper impact and help motivate you to continue to push yourself toward excellence. If you are willing to challenge yourself to master the skillset of being buttoned up, it will be a game changer for your career and reputation.

Chapter Summary

Lesson	How to Implement	When to Implement
Be Buttoned Up	• View your reputation as a brand you represent • Ask yourself if your response or expression is buttoned up (professional, to the point, and about the work, not the people) before reacting • Check in and check out of work • It doesn't matter what you say; it matters what the recipient hears • Mind your Ps and Qs • Talk about the work, not the person • Own it – your words, your actions, your reactions, and your expressions – own all of it	• Interacting with others • Using written communication • Coordinating work across stakeholders • Assigning work and reporting status

Chapter 5

Be Okay with Awkward Silence

If I had to choose my favorite piece of advice of all the wisdom my mentors shared over the years, "Be okay with awkward silence" would be it. With my tendency to be a people pleaser, I subconsciously ensured others felt comfortable around me. One way discomfort presented itself was in the form of a long, awkward silence in the workplace. While this advice was hard for me to incorporate into my routine, the benefits of following it were immediately apparent. I was unaware how much valuable information could be derived by simply keeping my mouth shut. I had already embraced the concept that my role was to listen and learn while I built up my skillset and experience, but this advice was different. It expanded my definition of what it means to listen and learn. I was absorbing as much information as possible when others spoke in meetings, presentations, conference calls, or even during impromptu discussions that occurred in hallways or at my desk. In my mind, once people stopped talking, there was no longer a need to listen and learn. Those moments of silence were filled with small talk about the weather or weekend plans, something I often initiated. I never viewed silence as an opportunity for others to say more until I heard this advice. If leveraged correctly, silence was a way to evolve and expand my knowledge base to the next level. I found that when the work conversation ended, and the silence crept in, my best learning occurred.

The reason valuable information can be derived during moments of silence is because the average person is conditioned to speak to alleviate the awkwardness and bring the conversation to closure. I found silence to be particularly awkward in one-on-one scenarios. The rule I followed to integrate this advice into my daily routine was simple: when there was nothing left to say, I stopped talking. It was harder to do than I expected. I had to bite my tongue a lot. I had to be very in tuned to the fact that I was intentionally integrating a new guideline into my work life and remind myself it was okay not to speak. When the awkward silence would sneak its way in, typically at the end of a conversation, I would think over and over, "Be okay with the silence, be okay with the silence..." And then it would happen. A few seconds after I recognized it was an awkward moment, the other person filled in the silence. Just as I was forcing myself to be quiet, the other person felt compelled to speak. There was nothing left to say, but they filled in the silence to avoid the uncomfortable feeling. Then the free information started to flow. With it came incredible insight and an understanding that anything the person chose to share, whether big or small, should not be repeated. It was up to them if they wanted to share with others and I knew they would respect and trust me more for understanding that, even if they never verbalized it. The direction each person chose to take the conversation varied. Sometimes when a person filled the silence, it was to share information about their personal life. I appreciated that type of knowledge because it provided me with a sharpened awareness and more accurate perception of the people I was working for and with. I would use the information to understand them better and adjust my approach to communicating, working, and engaging with them accordingly. It was great because I learned more about who my colleagues and stakeholders were naturally, not through prying or secondhand information.

Anytime I gained insight into colleagues and stakeholders, I viewed it as a treasured gift. The more I understood their emotional and intellectual state, what motivated them, what they appreciated most, how they preferred to communicate and why, the better off I was. It allowed me to not only improve my approach to working with that person, but also, they felt a stronger connection to me because they had been vulnerable and open with me. The person respected the unfortunately rare gift I had provided as well, a listening ear. As I interacted with more people and consciously made the effort to play the role of listener during awkward silences, I developed another skill. I learned how to read people. Specifically, I developed my abilities in terms of being aware of and playing off verbal and non-verbal cues. By listening, I had a rare opportunity to study another person and pick up on subtleties that provided me with an even deeper understanding of the thoughts, feelings, and actions of people in the workplace. I studied facial expressions, body language, tone of voice, and took cues based off the amount of information people shared. All these factors provided me with indirect feedback about how much the person agreed with me or cared about the conversation at hand. People told me, without using their words, how they perceived me and how invested they were in the work and the conversation.

It was essential to pay attention to these cues because it allowed me the opportunity to change my response accordingly. I could influence the outcome of the conversation by adjusting my words and tone based on the non-verbal cues I was getting. I could do it mid-conversation, and it enabled me to make forward progress with difficult people. For example, if someone looked down or away while I was speaking, I knew he or she was starting to lose interest. I would ask a clear and concise question in that moment, typically for their opinion, to re-direct and re-engage the person in the discussion. I had to practice that skill in order to develop it to that level, but it started with a desire to play the role of listener. It was easy to practice and develop daily because I was determined to be okay with awkward silence, and it seemed everyone else was more than willing to fill it in. I applied the skills I learned to meetings, presentations, and brainstorming sessions. Anytime I had an idea or solution to a problem and was collaborating with others,

I paused. I checked for non-verbal feedback and adjusted my approach accordingly. The more I learned to read people, the more fluid I was in my ability to pivot my response quickly, and the more influential I became.

Another category of information people used to fill awkward silences was their opinion on the work we were doing and other people's ideas. I do not mean workplace gossip, although some people chose to fill the silence that way. That was okay because it also gave me insight into who they were. However, most people filled in silences by stating their direct experiences at work. The type of experiences they described varied. It could be an experience with a new product the company was selling, a new software system we were mandated to use, a new process we were asked to follow, or a new person he or she had to work with or report to. People shared their experiences and opinions about collaboration, interaction, first impression, data collection and analysis, ideas on how to improve, and more. That information was priceless for me to acquire. It was especially helpful because I knew that sometimes people did not proactively share information I needed. Some people waited for me to ask the right question, but I didn't necessarily know what that was, particularly if I did not have a lot of visibility into that product, system, process, or person. However, when I was silent, information that I needed fell into my lap, and I didn't have to figure out the right question to ask. Or the information that fell into my lap made me realize which questions I had not asked but needed to.

I also began to understand the company I was working with much better. During those awkward silences, I learned about the person filling it in, but also about their connections, perceptions, and involvements with other tools, norms, and stakeholders. As time went on and I continued to collect perceptions from a wider variety of people who were filling in awkward silences, I started to develop a map in my mind of all the different preferences, backgrounds, connection points, opinions, and exchanges. I became a SME to go to for what and how to approach certain people and problems, all while gaining the trust and confidence of those who were sharing information. I was taken aback that I could experience so many benefits just by learning to keep my mouth shut and rejecting the impulse to speak. Most importantly, I realized that as it turns out, silence doesn't have to feel awkward.

Over time, I grew more and more knowledgeable about the people around me. In order to absorb it all and create a visual in my head, a map of sorts, that outlined everyone's interactions and preferences, I had to remember all of it. I would visualize my brain as a sponge. I would picture a giant, yellow sponge sopping up and absorbing everything – every word, non-verbal cue, reaction, and connection. All the data, blueprints, and comments seeped into my bright yellow sponge-like memory so I could reference it when needed. I felt like a police detective, slowly putting together my visual of people, considerations, and connections. I took pieces of all the stories and slowly mapped them together. I started to see how everything worked, who to ask different categories of questions, and how to draw accurate conclusions when only fragments of information were available.

The technique of visualization to improve memory muscle worked well for me. However, it was not the only thing I did to build that muscle. In order to remember most of the information I was acquiring, I had to possess a genuine interest in those I was working with and for. It was easy for me because it is innate. I am naturally fascinated by human behavior but realize that for others, it's a learned trait. Some people don't put the effort into even pretending they're interested in a conversation. Others don't see the value in listening, observing, and remembering information about the people who work next to them every day. It's a strength that needs to be built and involves a lot of effort. It requires putting any ego or agenda to the side, staying focused on another person for a long period of time, and buying into the idea that you can learn a lot from others, regardless of tenure, titles, or where they sit within the organization.

I had to understand and buy into the concept that knowing those around me would help me in my quest to build a stronger reputation. The people side of the organization needed my time and attention. Making time for it was a great way to ensure I was never bored; but I also recognized what I was getting was much bigger than that. Knowing others' preferred workstyles, being able to read people, putting together a map of dependencies and connections, and being able to see the big picture helped me to move up in the organization and achieve my career goals faster. That made me truly appreciate and grasp how much growth I was getting by really hearing what someone had to say.

Operating from that belief system enabled me to keep a genuine interest in those around me. I knew that if my interest in what my colleagues had to say was not genuine, they would pick up on it, so I had to find a way to ensure listening to them was something I appreciated. I saw the organization as a puzzle I had to put together and used systems thinking to depict each layer. When applying systems thinking, the macro-system is the entire organization, and the first layer of micro-system within it is the departments or functions, such as HR, IT, operations, logistics, supply chain, manufacturing and so on and so forth. The next micro-system layer within that is teams. For example, some of the teams that make up an HR function are payroll, benefits, talent acquisition, and diversity & inclusion. There is typically another micro-group within each team. For example, the payroll team may be divided into sub-groups who support different regions or functions. The next layer is the very first micro-level within the organization. That is the individual person and role they fill. This train of thought clarifies that each person is a piece of the puzzle for the macro-system, or organization, as a whole. If an organization is run by people with all types of backgrounds, skillsets, interests, behaviors, and personalities, then understanding them is the only way to comprehend all of the inner workings.

Learning the inner workings of an organization was a way for me to add more value. Adding more value was the best way for me to be seen, heard, and well-respected across the organization. Therefore, it served me to understand each layer of the organization because it made me more knowledgeable, skilled, and trusted. It carried invaluable benefits such as power and respect. By thinking of each role as a piece of the larger puzzle, I understood that I had to build familiarity with all the pieces if I wanted to see the full picture. There of course were numerous other benefits to buying into the belief that a genuine interest in the people I worked with was important. The people who made up each organization I worked for taught me a lot. Many times, they taught me how to do something, and other times they taught me how not to do it. Either way, the lessons were powerful. People were my greatest sources of learning about a company and how it worked. If I sought to add value through learning and focused on building my brand, then studying people who made up the organization was a key challenge I had to take on.

One difficult aspect of becoming the listener was finding the balance between putting effort into the people side of the organization while still completing my work on time. There were many days that I needed to get work done and could not sit and listen to conversations that ran long. Sometimes when people approached me, the thought that I needed to get back to my desk and start working consumed me. I was not able to listen in those moments. I realized that because I took on the role of listener by choosing not to speak in moments of silence, people sought me out to catch up in the hallways or swung by my workspace. I needed to find ways to draw boundaries. I always stopped and made eye contact and listened to people, even when I did not have time. That was the non-verbal cue I gave to validate the speaker. Through learning to read people, I became acutely aware of my own verbal and non-verbal cues and began to intentionally provide them to people. One of the cues I wanted to deliver was a way to politely remove myself from a conversation without offending or upsetting the person who was speaking. That was my way of setting the boundary. I wanted other people to know when I was and was not available to talk. When someone approached me, the conversation typically started with them greeting me and asking how I was doing. I recognized that as an opportunity to draw awareness to my boundary and provide a verbal cue. I began to respond, "I'm okay, but today is unfortunately a big deadline for me," or "A little stressed – I'm slammed today," or "Super busy – I'm in and out of meetings all day." Whatever the case, it tipped off the person that I did not have a lot of time to chat from the very beginning. The response I got was usually someone stating they would keep it short by jumping into a quick update or providing a summary before moving on. In moments when I didn't have an opportunity to set a boundary at the beginning of the conversation, or the person did not pick up on my verbal cue, I would wait for a pause and say, "Hey, I'm so sorry, I have to run," and provide a brief explanation such as, "I'm late to my next meeting," or "I have to pick up my daughter from school," or "I promised Sue I would get her my presentation in the next hour." I was never met with a rude response or even an offended look; it was always an apology for keeping me and a quick goodbye. If I could, I would respond, "Thank you so much. Hopefully we can catch up soon."

I always preferred to hear whatever story or information was being shared, but sometimes I truly didn't have the time. Preparing for those moments by identifying a set of go-to phrases in order to politely remove myself from a conversation was key. It was also another aspect of the advice I received to mind my Ps and Qs. If I said something that could be interpreted as dismissive, I needed to use words like "please" or "thank you" to soften the blow. It took effort to ensure I did not offend someone by walking away in the middle of a discussion. Over time, I adjusted my go-to phrases to fit my understanding of each person's communication style and proactively cater my response to fit that individual's preference. It became part of strengthening my memory muscle. I learned to expand my list of go-to phrases and used what suited my audience best in the moment.

Another helpful factor was that not every person filled every awkward silence that presented itself in the workplace. There were times when I had something to say in response and participated equally in the conversation. Sometimes there was no silence. The conversation flowed the entire time, then ended. These exceptions coupled with my go-to phrases helped me maintain a daily balance between completing work and learning about people and connections. Turning my focus to completing work was a welcome break, as it allowed my memory to take days off from absorbing and remembering so much information. Likewise, taking a break from getting work done at my desk to focus on listening and learning about the people side and connections across the organization was a nice way to unplug and step away from a deliverable I had been engrossed in. Balancing the two enabled me to mentally engage better in both areas. I would revisit a deliverable and see it differently and be able to improve it because I had walked away. Spending time focused on completing work made me better equipped to remember personal facts and preferences when awkward silences crept in and an opportunity to learn more about the people side of the organization presented itself.

The ability to find comfort in silence was a simple pivot from my innate instinct that brought significant benefits and learning opportunities. This allowed me to progress faster along my career path. It brought out information that I otherwise never would have been privy to. The most difficult part was learning to go against my natural tendency to fill an awkward silence by coaching myself to remain quiet and not feel compelled to speak. The most surprising aspect of this advice was how much others respected and trusted me for being silent and offering a listening ear. Before hearing this advice, I always thought I needed to do or say something to earn trust and respect. After implementing this advice, I learned that was not the case. Earning the trust and respect of others bestowed a great gift upon me: power. That can be a dangerous thing if not used wisely. I had to respect those who spoke in moments of awkwardness by not repeating their experiences and opinions to others. It was not my place to share information on their behalf. It was my place to use the information to better myself. It helped me grow my knowledge by putting the pieces of the overall puzzle together. It also helped me ask better questions and come up with better solutions because I had more insight into how things worked and what people liked and disliked about the project, processes, technology, cultural norms, and more.

Be willing to explore the people side of the organization. Understand that willingness and openness to trying new things is what allows you to acquire the knowledge necessary to stand out above the rest. Don't feel compelled to respond in moments of awkward silence. Learn how to sit comfortably in silence. That is the first step to gaining the insight and knowledge needed to build a strong reputation and become a powerful force within an organization. Then learn how to listen not only to what is being said, but what is not being said. Pick up on the tone people use, the level of interest they have about certain subjects, and their facial expressions when you share ideas, concerns, and solutions. Recognizing and remembering these cues helps you develop the skill of reading people. The ability to read people helps you to become an influencer within an organization. Influencers have the potential to leave the greatest impact on an organization because they directly affect business solutions and outcomes.

Chapter Summary

Lesson	How to Implement	When to Implement
Be Okay with Awkward Silence	• When there is nothing left to say, stop talking • Resist the urge to speak in moments of silence • Listen and learn, and absorb the information others share • Learn to read people by picking up on verbal and non-verbal cues • Be intentional about the verbal and non-verbal cues you provide others • Know there is power in learning the people side of an organization • Use systems thinking to depict parts of an organization • Have a list of go-to phrases to politely remove yourself from conversations	• Meetings/presentations • One-on-one conversations • Any time you are collaborating and interacting with teams and groups

Chapter 6

Don't Avoid Failure, Minimize Its Impact

Early on in my career as a management consultant, I had a client who was always terribly busy. She hired me to help her launch an internal marketing campaign for a new product her company was releasing. The goal was to build excitement among employees regarding the launch, and we were one workstream out of ten that supported a larger, worldwide marketing campaign. I had been staffed on the project for a couple of weeks, and we still had not announced our intent or determined our approach. We had missed our deadline. Even though I was supposed to manage our timeline, I didn't take any action when the deadline came and went. Not because I did not care or notice – it was because I did not know how to move things along. I tried to be patient while I waited for direction. I needed guidance to avoid any pitfalls, or worse, to avoid blame or getting fired because something went wrong.

One day I was on the phone with Stanley, my assigned manager. It was our weekly check-in, a time I used to report progress and ask any questions. I informed Stanley that the next step was for the client to announce our internal marketing campaign to the team who would help us launch it. He asked what I had done to get the work kicked off. I told him I didn't own defining the work. Due to this, I was spending my time learning about the client's organization by exploring the company intranet, reviewing documents she sent me, and meeting with other consultants who were staffed at the same company. He wanted to know why I hadn't started building intellectual property for the client to review or proactively scheduled time with her to discuss our plan. I explained that since it was my first project, I was unsure how to move things forward without my client's guidance. I had never participated in a marketing campaign. I'd never worked for her company. I didn't have any ideas or information that I could write down and show her. There was nothing I could do. Furthermore, I didn't want to set her up for failure or make a fool of myself by pitching a bad idea, making a wrong decision, or misadvising her. Stanley repeated his question. I paused, realizing my answer did not suffice. He said, "What are you doing to get the work complete?" I was silent. Then he said, "Why can't you move forward? Are you afraid to make a mistake?" I hesitated to respond. There was another long pause. I was searching for my words but could not find them. I didn't know how to explain myself. I heard Stanley take a breath. He broke the silence and said, "If you're holding back because you're scared to fail, stop it. Let me take your fear away by telling you this, *you will fail*. It will happen. Everyone fails at some point."

I remember being grateful we were on the phone so he couldn't see how taken aback I was. I didn't have a response. I was not sure what was holding me back. I genuinely thought I couldn't make any forward progress without guidance and coaching, so I didn't try. Maybe I was scared. As these thoughts raced through my head, Stanley continued, "It's not about avoiding failure – it's about minimizing the impact when you do fail. It's about learning how to take chances and trust your gut." I wasn't quite sure how to do that, but I wanted to learn.

I realized quickly that my own expectation about how I should be set up for success was my first misstep. My assumption was some type of training would be provided because I didn't know how to add value if no one onboarded me. Initially I found myself upset and frustrated by the lack of training and guidance. Since I couldn't do anything about it, I thought the best thing to do was follow my client's lead. Stanley was telling me the expectation was that I performed well despite the ambiguity I was faced with. If I couldn't do that, I wasn't the right fit for the job. I had to let go of the idea that someone would guide me through my new role. I had to accept that I was responsible for making forward progress even though I was new and inexperienced. That meant I had to let the fear of making a mistake go and identify effective techniques to navigate my way through ambiguous circumstances. The only way I could do that was if I expected and accepted failure as part of my learning process.

In my quest to minimize the impact of failure, I realized that there was a direct correlation between failure and ambiguity. The more ambiguity, the higher the chance of failure. That meant I needed techniques to decrease the amount of ambiguity in order to decrease the risk of failure. I found myself in an ambiguous situation because I was at a new company, in a new role, and owning a new initiative I had no experience with. Once I unpacked what led to failure, I was ready to learn how to better manage it. I did not want to learn how to survive ambiguity. I wanted to learn how to thrive in it. Thriving in ambiguity meant proactively identifying roles, particularly my own, as well as dependencies, processes, expectations, and stakeholders. Then I needed to know how everything fitted together. The only way to do that was one step at a time. I had to be willing to take the first step toward progress in the absence of knowing and understanding everything, or anything at all really.

The first step was adjusting how I thought about the situation. I had to accept that when I joined a new organization, took on a new role, or owned a new book of work and did not receive training or guidance, it didn't make me a victim or unable to move forward. It meant I was trusted enough to figure it out. I had to view it as a compliment and challenge myself to overcome the ambiguity. I learned to push myself to the point where I was comfortable with ambiguity. Stanley used to say, "Remember that it's not what happens to you – it's how you respond." It was true. Leadership, mentors, colleagues, clients, and other employees were aware I was dealing with ambiguity and unpleasant problems because they were also dealing with their own set of issues. Customers expected that I would rise to the occasion and solve issues before they reached them. Everyone knew that I would have to deal with problems, foreseen and unforeseen, at work. What they didn't know was how I would respond in the moment. People were quietly watching in the background to see how I navigated my way through. That meant time spent dwelling on what happened or why was wasted energy. I had to focus my energy on how I responded to the challenge because that revealed the real value I brought to the table.

I found the best way to navigate ambiguity was to schedule time with my client, the person accountable for the project's success, and proactively understand the following attributes of my work initiative: who, what, where, why, when, and how. My first step on every project was to schedule 2 to 3 hours of time to clarify the answers to those questions. If I wanted to minimize the chance of failure, I needed to answer those questions before I could take any action. The how question, as in how we approached and completed the work, was often something we had a loose idea of but needed to clarify further as we progressed. The rest of those questions – who, what, where, why, and when – had answers. In order to alleviate some of the ambiguity, I needed to know those answers. I usually had a general idea of what we were doing, though I needed to drill down, but I typically started by answering the who question: who were we working with and for? I needed to understand the names and roles of those who were on our team or had a stake in our work. The what question complemented both the who and the why, and there were a few aspects to it. The first was what impact our initiative would have on whom. The second was what was changing, meaning what we were doing currently versus what we would be doing in the future when we implemented the initiative. Similarly, I needed to understand why our initiative added value and was an improvement from the current state. The when question covered our timeline and key milestones. The where question also had a few aspects to it. I needed to know where the customers and stakeholder sat within the organization – departments, teams, and geographies – as well as their levels within the company. This complemented the other questions because in addition to knowing the names of the people we had dependencies on, I needed to know where they sat within the organization. I needed to understand if the portion of the work they owned was upstream or downstream from our portion, and what that meant in terms of how to partner together to achieve the desired outcome.

While I initially intended to onboard myself to new roles by clarifying the answers to each question, it turned out that this was information everyone needed to know. Typically, my client gave me the answers or realized she needed to go find out the answers after I asked. Once the answers were known, the client and I needed to share them with anyone who was participating in or affected by our book of work. Clarifying and agreeing to the answers to each of those questions helped us align and remove unnecessary ambiguity as a team. Once I understood the who, as in my customers, team members, and stakeholders, I would set up meet and greets with whomever the client thought could give me more insight or would be working closely with me. I spent the first 5 minutes of the meet and greets introducing myself and explaining how my role would interact with theirs. The rest of the time I used to learn about people's roles, responsibilities, availability, and perspectives on how to best partner. If I could, I tried to take the meetings a step further by watching for and observing verbal and non-verbal cues. I tried to pick up on any hints regarding preferred communication or workstyle so I could apply what I learned when interacting with them. That was how I consistently spent my first week or two on every new project I took on. It was my way of unpacking ambiguity, and it worked.

Once I began to expect ambiguity and learned to navigate it, I needed to understand how to minimize the impact of inevitable mistakes or errors that occurred down the line. In order to do this, I had to understand how the organization worked and where the connections lay. My visual was a game of Jenga. If I added or removed a piece, what happened to the rest of the structure? Did it fall or remain standing? I had to be sure I didn't move the piece that could bring the whole thing crashing down. That meant I had to understand the lay of the land, what the pieces in my Jenga game were, and how they were stacked. Managing risk impacts also started with knowing the who, what, where, why, when, and how attributes of the project. These questions removed ambiguity, but also clarified the connections and layers within the work. To manage the impact of any potential failures, I had to dig deeper into these questions and learn the detailed information that may not have been identified when we initially answered them at a high level. To build off the marketing campaign example, there were team members I was coordinating with as well as teams working alongside us. Each team, including mine, had a separate scope of work, but we were all managing different aspects of a broader initiative – a product launch campaign. We each had a target audience, and sometimes our audiences overlapped. My target audience was all employees who worked to develop the product that was being released. I had to think through each step of what we were doing and then think through who it would affect and how. To complete the marketing campaign, we needed to purchase signage, prizes, and party materials for teams to celebrate the product release across the globe. The steps we planned to take were to identify our budget, understand trade and legal guidelines, purchase and brand our swag, and identify a point of contact to coordinate a release party per country. As I clarified a more detailed answer to each question – who, what, where, why, when, and how – I began to see that each of those steps were my Jenga pieces. I knew what I had to do first and where the dependencies lay, which was how the Jenga pieces were stacked.

One of the biggest ways to combat failure is through communication. I knew what I needed to communicate to whom. I knew which communications were most essential and which were not, meaning which of the communication-based Jenga pieces could bring the whole thing crashing down if they were not sent in a timely manner and which would just leave the structure slightly tilted if they were delayed. Since I was jumping into details and understanding the dependencies at a much deeper level, I was also identifying when and how to partner with other groups that were leading a different initiative within the same broader product launch campaign, particularly if we had the same audience. I could collaborate with them to ensure we were not confusing our audience by sending too much information or any contradictory email announcements. To understand these nuances and where the dependencies were, I identified the business groups we worked with and met with the people who sat on those teams. I used tools like organizational charts, global address lists, meet and greets, and my client and colleague's tribal knowledge about a process or team to grow my own knowledge and identify the right points of contact.

Once I built my foundational knowledge from the client during my onboarding time, I used these tools to expand my knowledge. I asked detailed questions during meet and greets, which led me to set up more meet and greets with other people who my stakeholders recommended as knowledgeable resources. In some of those meetings, I clarified my understanding of the current state versus the future, or desired state, we were moving toward. That was the "what" question I summarized during my first meeting. Once I had met with everyone and learned all of the details and perspectives on the current and future states, I knew when something was a risk. As I acquired more and more knowledge about the details, I realized who a risk would impact and how. I began to rate risks in terms of their likelihood of occurring and the level of impact they could have. I asked myself, "If this happened, would it impact few or many and how badly?" I minimized the impact a risk could have by documenting and sharing it with the right people, then determining a mitigation plan if the risk did occur. There were still some blind spots where I had to trust my gut instinct and make a quick decision, but for the most part I had alleviated my fear of failure because I knew I was managing potential risks in a way that ensured their impact would be minimized.

Many times, ambiguity occurred without warning because a change was introduced, and its effects were either unknown or only partially known. Jill used to tell me the first emotion a human felt when faced with change was fear. It was important for me to recognize that for a few reasons. One was that in times when I represented the change, I needed to understand a natural fear was ignited in those impacted, and their instinct would be to avoid me. Due to the nature of my role as a consultant, I was joining a variety of initiatives and projects that were temporary. I was always launching or kicking off something new. Sometimes it was a welcomed initiative, like an internal marketing campaign. Other times, it was not welcomed, like implementing a new, mandatory software system. When I was assigned an initiative, or even a task, that forced others to change the way they worked, I knew my risk of failure increased because others were impacted, and success was dependent on their ability to accept change.

Learning and expecting others to follow *The Change Curve* was a key aspect of managing people-related risks (see Figure 1, page 82). *The Change Curve* was first documented in the 1960s by

Elisabeth Kubler-Ross to explain the grief process. Over time, it became a tool used by change management practitioners because the emotional process it depicted could also be applied to what happened when the workforce learned a change was going to affect their work life. Since the change was introducing ambiguity, and that was something many were uncomfortable with, people retaliated. They had to go through phases, like denial and anger, before they could get to acceptance. It was important for me to understand that process, so I was educated on recognizing when something was truly at risk. I needed to respect and accept the emotional process people went through but also educate myself so I could be proactive in my approach to managing change and helping others through ambiguity. Understanding this provided me with the reasoning behind others' reactions and helped me adjust my approach accordingly. When people made it to acceptance, it was my cue that we had survived. I realized that I also went through those stages when faced with ambiguity. I needed to be patient with myself during times of change. I had to realize that frustration and fear were part of the process. I had to go through those emotions in order to accept the change and thrive despite it. I trained myself to get through each phase quicker by recognizing when the process was occurring and consciously making the decision to be willing to learn and open to the idea that different could mean better. Giving myself and other people the space and time to go through the emotional side of ambiguity was a great way to gage and manage risk related to the people side of the organization. In addition, it helped me understand that in the beginning, when a change was announced, not all risks raised by stakeholders were rational. Sometimes a stakeholder identified a risk that ended up being something we did not need to solve for. It was actually just that person's way of delaying or avoiding change, and represented the stage of change that person was in – such as denial, anger, or bargaining. Once I learned *The Change Curve*, it wasn't difficult to recognize when someone was raising a realistic risk or one associated with their desire to avoid change. The real risks are hard to find solutions to. If someone is raising a risk related to a change and you can easily poke holes in the importance and impact of the risk, they are likely going through *The Change Curve*, and just require reassurance and validation.

One of the biggest failures I experienced in my career was sharing information without getting the proper permission. It happened 4 or 5 years into my profession. I shared one team's document with another without really thinking about how confidential it was. This caused a bit of an uproar. Stanley called me to discuss it, as the issue was escalated to him by a couple of my stakeholders. I felt upset and embarrassed in the moment, but it passed very quickly. The damage control I had to do was minimal. It was a quick apology and explanation of why to those who were upset, and then it was over. I learned from it. I never shared anything that was not my own again without asking the owner first, even if I thought it didn't matter. That was the funny thing about making mistakes. When I did fail, what I had done wrong was cemented so deeply in my brain that I never made the same mistake twice. Thanks to Stanley, when I did fail, the impact was so minimal that it was hardly noticed. I also was expecting failure to occur, so it was not something that threw me off or caused me so much distress I was unable to bounce back and re-focus on the task at hand. I noticed that when I expected to fail, it did not mean that I failed more often. In fact, because I had learned how to manage the impact of failure, it was a rare occurrence that was often not noticeable to others. I also took more risks because I removed my fear of failure. I never sat back and waited. I pushed ahead and if I needed to take a risk to get the ball rolling, I did so. I realized that the more I learned to expect and accept failure, the more fearless I became.

Stanley and I discussed the "so what?" of failure throughout my first project. I changed my belief system about failure. I went from trying to learn how to avoid failure to learning how to minimize the impact. I knew it was okay to fail because it was how I learned. One of the most important aspects of failure was learning how to forgive myself when I did make a mistake. One of Stanley's go-to phrases was, "Hindsight is 20/20." Anytime I made a mistake, it was easy to see how I could have done better. Everyone can see clearly from the rearview mirror. It's the windshield that's hard. I reminded myself of this when I made a mistake and worried that it was too big or important, or felt anxious about what others would think. I also learned to only look in the rearview mirror if it would help me learn from my mistakes and not to overly critique myself. I had to allow myself to fail, and I had to be patient and understanding with myself when I did.

It was naive of me to think I would navigate my career without failing. I realized the most profound learning would come from failure, and that was a gift. If I made a mistake but learned how to avoid it in the future, that was a win. It meant the next time I would make a different mistake and learn from that one. This would continue until I had acquired so much knowledge from my mistakes that failure became more and more rare. I had to tell myself that no one was watching me and thinking, or worse, *saying*, "She failed so we must get rid of her." I expected mistakes to occur because I knew everyone made them. I also realized that if I paid careful attention to the big stuff, the areas where I did fail would be forgotten. They were a small hiccup in the overall objective of the work, which I always met. When I made a mistake, if I owned it, people were understanding. They forgave and they forgot. I was the one who remembered, but I changed the way I reflected on my mistakes. I chose to focus on the learning I gained from them so I could be better.

Most people spend anywhere from 30 to 50 years of their

lives building a career. We experience a wide variety of learning moments during our careers, but over time, they fade, and only a few standout. Many people spend effort and energy avoiding any moment that resembles failure. However, if something teaches you to do and be better, then it is not a failure. In fact, allowing failure to occur and learning from it makes you a leader. Moments when failure occurs are what you will remember most because that will be where your greatest learning comes from. If you want to be ahead of the game, go into your career by expecting and accepting failure. Look forward to what failure will teach you. Focus your time and effort on learning how to manage and minimize the impacts of inevitable failures, so when you do fail, it's not a catastrophe – it's a lesson learned.

Chapter Summary

Lesson	How to Implement	When to Implement
Don't Avoid Failure, Minimize Its Impact	• Expect and accept failure as part of the learning process; remember that everyone makes mistakes • Be comfortable with ambiguity • Tell yourself it's not about what happens to you, it's how you respond • Be able to answer the following questions regarding your work: who, what, where, why, when, and how • Document the current and desired state • Document risk probability and impact levels (high, medium, and low scale) • Be aware that the first emotion humans feel when they know change is coming is fear • Learn the change curve and apply it in ambiguous settings • When you do inevitably fail or make a mistake, find out why and how so you can avoid it in the future	• In a new role or when owning new responsibilities • Implementing or launching a new initiative, project, or program • When providing project or change management services

Figure 1: Kubler-Ross Change Curve

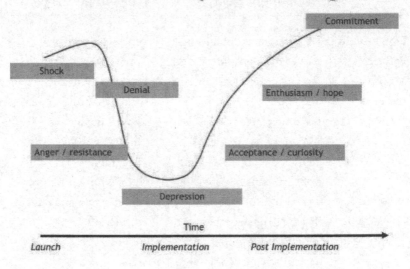

Kubler-Ross, E., 1969. Kubler-Ross model of change. Change Curve available at: <https://silverlobster.files.wordpress.com/2015/09/kubler-ross-change-curve-001.jpg> [accessed 2 February 2022].

Chapter 7

Don't Try to Understand Why If You Can't Influence It

Throughout my career, I put a lot of focus and energy into observing others and seeking out ways to learn and evolve. I aimed to develop my skillset, approach, and reputation based on my observations and learnings. That meant I was taking in a lot of information that needed to be sorted through. I needed guidance on the best way to manage and catalog so much data. I needed a way to know what was worth my time in terms of self-reflection, analysis, and understanding. I didn't want to agonize over work situations unnecessarily, but I also didn't want to miss an opportunity to improve my brand or skillset. Jill pointed out that I shouldn't focus my time and attention on things that couldn't be influenced. She said I didn't need to understand why something happened if I could not influence or change the outcome. While I didn't immediately understand how to apply her advice, it became much clearer once I started to ask myself the question, "Is this something I can influence?" I was taken aback by the realization that the way to become an influential person was to first understand what I could *not* influence. Forcing myself to become aware of what I couldn't influence yielded many benefits, such as work-life balance, the ability to quickly and easily prioritize, understanding the importance of defining and abiding by agreed upon roles and responsibilities, and the ability to easily disengage after a long day. I learned to stay in my lane and not overstep boundaries. If I was not the owner of something, I was acutely aware of that fact and acted as such. If a decision, direction, or announcement was made that I disagreed with, I asked myself if I could influence the outcome and change what I disagreed with. If the answer was no, then I didn't try. It was freeing. I felt lighter in my day-to-day because it took the pressure off. Jill's advice was what I needed. It put guardrails around where and how to focus my time and energy.

One of the first things Jill pointed out to me as something I could *not* influence was a job offer after I completed an interview process. As a management consultant, I had to interview with the client company for each project I was staffed on. I was the type of person who struggled with intense nerves before job interviews. I felt shaky and got a knot in the pit of my stomach. It affected my ability to concentrate and feel confident. When I was interviewing for one of my first roles, I told Jill how nervous I was. She said there was nothing to be nervous about – either I was the right fit, or I wasn't. She went on to explain why it didn't need to go deeper than that. Her point was that interviewees could not control the final outcome. I was over-complicating the process by thinking that my ability to interview well was the primary driver in the decision. That was the wrong viewpoint. My viewpoint should have been that if I had the right skillset and was a good cultural fit, then the role would be mine. If not, then it was the wrong role for me. "Remember, you're interviewing them too," Jill explained. I was part of the decision with regard to role fit. I was determining if it was a fit just as much as the employer. She was right. The interview process was just two parties coming together to determine fit, and we had equal say. I had more power from that viewpoint. It made my perspective shift from "I really hope they like me" to "I really hope I like them."

I also realized that if I thought it was a great fit, but the interviewers disagreed, there was nothing I could do. It was a waste of my time to agonize over things. It meant some other interviewee was an even better fit than me, and that was okay. Once I shifted my mindset to align with Jill's explanation, I grasped that I could influence fit only to a point. I could ask about the role requirements in my interview to learn more, so I had the information I needed to make my decision. I could also provide the interviewers with examples of what I had done previously that showed where I was the right fit during the interview. But that's where my influence ended. Once I could see that, I was able to flow with the interview process and final decisions, instead of trying to control the outcome. I noticed my presence shifted as well. When I interviewed for a new role, I was more confident because I felt empowered. I was curious and excited because I was clear on what I could and could not influence. I became eager for the part of the interview where I was asked if I had questions. That was my opportunity to interview them and participate in the decision about fit. I wanted to use it appropriately and had to put thought into what to ask. How did things really work? What was the culture like? What was the best and most difficult thing about working there? What types of obstacles did people face? After the interview, during the awkward time where I waited for a decision, I used to struggle. I silently critiqued myself, analyzing every detail of my interview performance. After Jill's advice, I changed. I used that time to think about my part of the decision. Did the employer I interviewed with seem like the right fit for me? Were those the type of people who I wanted to work alongside every day? I took the decision so seriously, that if I wasn't sure about fit, I would think, "Well, if they say no, at least I won't have to worry that I'm making the wrong decision," and that was a world away from my previous approach. It alleviated the burden I felt when I saw the situation under the new lens Jill provided. Once I knew my role and how to participate, I was never nervous about an interview again. If I didn't get the job, then it wasn't the right place for me. The details didn't matter. It wasn't worth my time to try and figure out why because nothing I did would change the outcome. I couldn't influence it. I knew something else would come along that would be the right fit, and that's where I chose to focus my time and effort.

I started to apply this thinking when I interviewed others as well. I worried less about pinpointing what needed to change to make them a fit. I didn't put thought into whether a potential hire could be coached and trained to become a right fit. I focused on whether they were a fit in that moment, without training, coaching, or guidance. If they were not a good fit, it just meant they were intended to fill a different role where their skillsets could be better utilized. That was a good thing for both parties. The best thing to do when a person and a job don't fit together is to say it and move on. I let go of any false beliefs I had that I needed to understand why. If job fit couldn't be influenced, then there was no point in trying to understand the reasoning behind the decision.

Another way to identify what could not be influenced was to understand my role versus the roles of those I collaborated with – specifically, knowing each role's level of accountability and who was responsible for what. As a management consultant assigned to different roles with different companies, I was always the responsible party. My client was always the accountable party. It was important for me to know who the accountable party was in everything I did. As the responsible party, I was doing the bulk of the work, but was not the individual held accountable by the organization for the outcome. My clients were the people held accountable because they were employees of the company, and they were paying me to help them. Whatever outcome my client and I were responsible for, they were assigned that work and hired me as part of the team who would help them complete it. The accountable party in every workplace scenario is the person held accountable for the outcome by executive leadership.

A professor in graduate school gave me some great advice regarding how to view my role as the *responsible* party versus that of the *accountable* party. She said, "Never care more than your client." This advice became a mantra I repeated to myself often when learning to disengage from what I couldn't influence. The word "client" could be replaced with whomever the accountable party was, or the owner of the work, such as your manager or supervisor. The advice translates to *the responsible party should never care more than the accountable one*. As I put this advice into practice, I realized how important it was to align my effort and buy-in level to that of the accountable party. When the accountable party communicated the chosen path and deeply bought in to that idea, it meant I couldn't influence it. If someone who was *not* the accountable party bought into a path we should take, it could still be influenced. It was only when the owner of the work was firm in their stance on the direction we would follow or a decision we would respect that I had to let go of anything that was not aligned to that direction or decision. Likewise, if the accountable party were disinterested in something, I could easily influence it. I didn't have to put effort into influencing the details that the client was indifferent to. Often, I could own decisions and directions regarding those variables. I learned to move those types of variables along quickly. If I was focused on variables the accountable party didn't put any emphasis on, then I cared more than my client, and that was what I wanted to avoid. It didn't serve me to spend significant time and effort trying to understand or dig deep on something the accountable party never cared about. For every project I was staffed on, I aligned the level of effort I put into something to the depth of care the owner, or accountable party, had for the outcome.

There were inevitably times when I disagreed with the owner of the work or foresaw problems in the direction the owner took. The best I could do in those situations was share my concerns, in terms of risks and mitigations, with the owner. Sometimes the accountable party changed course or direction based on what I shared. Sometimes they did not. Either way, I had done my job. As the responsible party, I was an advisor and a doer. If I advised, and the client did not listen, it didn't mean I was no longer the doer. In instances where my client would not change course even after listening to risks, I had to let go of my concerns and move on. Caring more than the accountable party and putting up a fight to do something was a waste of my time and effort. I was not the owner of the work, so why act like I was by fighting about the go-forward plan? I learned to let the owners do what they thought best and be content with knowing I did my job by surfacing risks. The way I saw it, I had two choices. I could sulk and fight the path we were moving on or I could get on board with the solution and help move it forward. Once I knew that it was a waste of my time to try to understand that which could not be influenced, I chose to help move the solution forward. Once again, I learned to flow with the work and decisions, instead of trying to control something I didn't own.

I observed many colleagues' and stakeholders' frustrations and anger over an owner's decision or direction they disagreed with. I witnessed them trying to force a change. They would unnecessarily bring other people into the conversation, raise the issue at inappropriate times, or try to go above the accountable party to a supervisor. These attempts to sabotage were a waste of time that ended badly for the saboteur. Anyone who tried to influence something they didn't own became overly involved emotionally and unable to stay in a healthy and clear mindset while doing their work. The result was their work and reputation suffered – all because they cared too much about how someone else was doing their job. It was a bit of an epidemic in the workplace that people couldn't let other people own their mistakes and failures. Even if the owner of the work were wrong in the direction they chose to take, the worst that would happen is they would fail. If that happened, they would be the ones held accountable for the failure, which meant they would learn from it. I never wanted to be a blocker to someone else's learning. I knew people experienced their greatest lessons through failures and I wanted to give them the space and time to do so. That was another reason I never cared more than the owner of the work. My time was precious and fleeting, so I could not waste it. Instead of dwelling on what I could not affect, I asked myself, "Where can I have the most impact?" I turned my attention to answering that question. That was how I ensured my energy, time, focus, and effort were purposeful and useful. I knew my ideas and proposed solutions should be aimed only where I could have the most impact because that was how I added the most value.

One fascinating observation I made was that even when I disagreed with a decision or plan the accountable party made, it often worked out anyway. After that happened a couple of times, I recognized what it meant. There were many paths to get to an outcome and just because we were not on my preferred path didn't mean the desired outcome wouldn't be achieved. From that perspective, there was a lot to be learned by getting on board with a decision that I disagreed with. It was a great opportunity for me to observe the obstacles and enablers along a different path to an outcome, especially one that I'd never tried before, did not initially think was best, or never would have thought of. Sometimes the path I disagreed with turned out to be the best one to the outcome. It meant I was wrong in my initial assessment. Some of my best learning came from those scenarios. During the many times I disagreed with a decision, I reminded myself that it didn't mean I was right, and the other person was wrong. That wasn't even what mattered. What was important was not my opinion – it was how I spent my time and effort once a decision I could not influence was made. Whether the decision was minor, like the color of paper to print an employee pamphlet on, or major, like expanding the target audience for a system implementation, I needed to recognize when I could no longer influence it.

Part of what made differentiating between what I could and could not influence difficult was that sometimes it changed. Many times, I could influence a variable initially or to a point, but then something would change. An executive would have an opinion, or an issue would come up that put our work on the back burner or delayed the timing of when we could implement. Then the information we had was no longer applicable, and we had to start from scratch or accept a new path, and the variable could no longer be affected. When that happened and a new decision was made unexpectedly, I also had to let it go. I disliked it, but I couldn't influence it and therefore could not give any of my limited time, effort, or attention to it. I had to set and stick to boundaries. Anything that couldn't be influenced didn't require my clear understanding of why it was happening. It required something else: my alignment and buy-in despite my level of agreement. Knowing when it was necessary to understand the reason and strategy behind a decision or direction versus when I needed to accept it without debate allowed me to focus my determination and attention in the right place. I always asked myself, "Can I influence this?" when I felt nervous or upset over something that happened in my work life. If the answer was yes, I would dig into the how. I would think through every aspect of the problem, determine the outcome I hoped to achieve, and build a case for the approach I thought was best. If the answer was no, there was no additional action to take. That meant I saved myself a lot of time and brain power by just accepting the circumstance I was in. I could then focus my effort somewhere that mattered. Somewhere that I could influence.

After I mastered how to identify what could and could not be influenced, I wanted to take the next step. I wanted to learn how to be influential. There were two pieces of advice that helped frame my approach to influencing. The first came from Stanley. He told me, "The only thing that really matters is whether or not you meet your objective." That advice simplified how I knew if I had influenced something and where to focus my effort. It meant I needed to be able to clearly articulate my objective and purpose when I facilitated a meeting, completed a task, or identified a go-forward plan. One way I held myself accountable to meeting my objective was in my communications, such as emails, conversations, or meetings. In my position, I coordinated several meetings and often determined the agenda. Scheduling meetings for the sake of having meetings was a popular issue I experienced across many teams, departments, and companies. It was one of my biggest pet peeves because it wasted everyone's time and discouraged people from attending any meetings at all. One way I influenced attendance and outcomes was to document one to three concisely written objectives and include them in meeting invites. I wanted everyone to be crystal clear on the purpose of the meeting and what we came to decide or discuss. The meeting objective was typically a decision that needed to be made, but it could also be a request to review a deliverable or decision, sharing status and risks, an announcement, or launching new work. My meetings only ended in one of two ways. The first was we ran out of time, which meant we needed to either schedule more time or determine why we were unable to meet the objectives and revisit the game plan. The second was that we met our objectives. If we crossed off each objective in the meeting and still had time left, I would say, "We're done. If there are no questions, we can end this call" and give people their time back. I never wanted to encourage people to stray from the objectives, which drove the agenda topics. I wanted them to know that if I could use even one second less of their time to achieve the objectives, I would. I never had a meeting without purpose. When attendees began to take us off topic, I would say, "Let's place these points in the parking lot and revisit them another day." The "parking lot" was a popular term used in structured meetings to describe the action of documenting off-topic agenda items to be revisited at another time. It was extremely important to have a term like parking lot. I needed somewhere to put off-topic agenda items to ensure I had dedicated time to achieve the objectives I outlined. Having a game plan for managing related topics that didn't help move us toward the meeting objectives was another important tool for influencing the conversation, and it was something I could fully own.

Running meetings efficiently and effectively kept everyone on track. It was a way for me to influence team alignment and the pace at which the work unfolded and was completed. I became good at it – so good that I thought no one could throw a meeting I was running off course. Until one day when I attended a 4-hour meeting I had scheduled with my client's legal team. We were expanding their product from a national offering to a global one and had several questions that needed to be answered. From the moment we sat down, my meeting was hijacked by the lawyers in the room, and I panicked. I thought about my objectives. I had several. The meeting was 4 hours, so I planned on uncovering a lot of information. If we were going to expand the sale of a product into multiple foreign countries, I had a lot of detailed questions about the local laws in each country and what we needed to be aware of or plan for. As I sorted through the details in my head, I realized the first requirement to expand globally was to get the legal team's approval to do so. That meant even if I could not get details, I just needed a yes or no, a thumbs up or down for us to move forward. We could get into the details later. I also realized that the details would be better to clarify in a one-on-one setting once I saw how they all interacted and dominated the conversation. Anytime there was a pause in the conversation, I asked, "What information do you need to make a decision on global expansion?" and waited anxiously for a clear, concise response. Each time, one lawyer would look up at all the other attorneys and say, "Well, we would need to consider this issue" and launch into a detailed, philosophical discussion about some random law that I couldn't clearly link to my question or our meeting objectives. The conversation would take many twists and turns until they were debating something totally different than global expansion, or so it seemed to me. When another pause occurred, I asked the same question again. Another lawyer would speak up with a similar response as the last but bring up a slightly different law or variable they should consider. This cyclical pattern continued. I watched the clock as the legal team seemed to discuss every international business law ever made and answer hypothetical questions that no one except them seemed to understand. I tried to insert questions that I thought would lead us to the objective. I thought about how to influence the discussion. I tried everything I could think of and the next time I looked up at the clock, I realized there were only 5 minutes left of the 4 hours I scheduled. I interrupted the conversation and called out a few of the lawyers by name. They looked up at me as I asked what their decision would be – thumbs up or down – based on that day's conversation. They paused and then one of them said, "My decision would be yes, thumbs up." The others nodded their heads in agreement.

My client was sitting next to me and threw his arms in the air in celebration while looking at me in disbelief. The day before, he warned me that the legal team was a difficult group, and their ability to form a consensus was mediocre at best. I had dismissed the warning because I thought as long as I took control of the meeting agenda and guided the conversation, we could overcome that issue. I had not anticipated I would be unable to guide the conversation, but I was excited because I knew I did the only thing that mattered. I met my objective. If Stanley had not clarified what my end goal should be, I wouldn't have known what to do. I would have wasted time thinking about how I could have controlled that conversation better. Half the time I had no idea what anyone was saying because I didn't speak their attorney language fluently enough. I lost all control of the meeting about 2 minutes in. I had an agenda for us to review each country we hoped to expand into, but we never discussed any of it. My usual "parking lot" trick didn't work because they were having such a technical discussion, I didn't know if it was off topic or not, nor was I given an opportunity to break in other than the random pauses where all I could sneak in was, "So, can we move forward?" But when I realized that I hit my objective, I knew it was a success. The first 3 hours and 55 minutes didn't matter – only those last 5 minutes. Regardless of how long it took, I did what was needed to make forward progress. Afterwards, I followed up with the attorneys individually based on the countries they represented and got the detailed questions answered as well. It was not the path I planned, but in the end, all of my objectives were met. This happened because I took the time to get really clear and crisp on what I needed to know. During the 4-hour meeting, I poured my effort and thought processes into how to pull out just that one piece of information. I didn't have to question what it was I needed to do to influence our solution and meeting outcome. I already knew that if I could achieve the primary objective, it was a success.

The other piece of advice that helped me learn how to influence came from a colleague. I asked her my favorite question, "What's the best advice you ever received in your career?" She spoke of the important skill of being able to influence others. Specifically, she said, "Sell your idea, don't argue your point." She explained that this depended on one's ability to steer conversations and present ideas in a way that led everyone toward their desired outcome. She said the people who were most skilled at influencing often had an idea that they allowed others to realize on their own. People thought something the influencer had thought of was their original idea and then pitched it to their colleagues when in all actuality, the influencer had led the person to that thought in hopes they would buy into the idea and help the influencer get others on board with it.

I found a couple of ways to do this. The first was to ask questions. When I disagreed with a path, as long as the decision was still in process, I could inquire about the approach. I grasped that when I asked specific questions about my concern, the decision-maker realized on their own the same issue I had already foreseen. One example of this is when I was working on a software implementation and disagreed with what the draft email entailed in announcing the work. It announced what we were doing, but not why, when, or who to contact. I knew all of those questions would arise when the intended audience of ~1500 employees received the email. However, neither myself nor the client drafted the email. My client was allowed to give input into the draft, but I was not. In a one-on-one meeting with my client, she briefly referenced the announcement email, stating it would go out in a few days and then the hard work would begin. I asked her who we should point people to for questions. She looked back over the email and said "Huh, I'm not sure who is on point. It doesn't say." I responded by asking if she thought we should include someone, and she enthusiastically said yes and that she would point this out to the owner of the draft. I followed up by asking if we were including a timeline or outlining key benefits in the announcement or if that was something we should follow up with. Again, she wanted it included in the announcement. I never found out why that information was missing from the initial draft or how my client had previously missed it, but it didn't matter. I asked questions and found that it was something they wanted to fix. I didn't have to revise it or get involved. I just simply asked the right question, and the outcome I hoped for was achieved. Learning how to ask the right questions is a powerful skillset, and one that anyone who hopes to be influential must learn to master.

The second way I incorporated this advice was through presentations I gave. I had to put more time into thinking through why my idea was appealing and what about it would entice another person to advocate for it. I had to know my audience in order to sell them something. Every time I created a deliverable or presented an idea or solution to someone or a group of people, I thought, "Who is my audience, and how will they perceive this?" I had to think through any questions my audience might have, what would confuse them, and whether the data and evidence to support my conclusion were clear. I had to simplify what I wanted to say and the reason for my recommendation. Simplifying it was the way to remove complexity, which removed confusion. If I made the evidence for my recommendation simple and clear, then the person I was pitching it to would come to the same conclusion I had on their own.

Thinking through and weighing all these questions and elements took time. It also resulted in multiple revisions of my work before socializing it, which required extra effort and focus. I made the decision to put the extra work in upfront because I knew it was time well spent and would save me time and energy down the line. The result was consistent. My audience bought what I was selling. They were sold on my idea, solution, or recommendation. I sharpened my skillset the more I practiced and soon, anytime someone had a question, I had already thought of it, so it was easy to respond. Since I accounted for my audience's concerns and questions ahead of time and often proactively addressed them in my presentation or argument, it was easy for people to buy into my idea. If I had not thought through each person's perspective, questions, and concerns, then I would have been arguing my point. My pitch, presentation, or argument would have been something that only represented my ideas and questions. It would have been something I had to defend. That was not what I wanted. That was not the way to influence. My work had to be something I was offering, and people needed to be able to digest its value without a lot of effort or debate. I understood that rarely if ever will anyone buy-in to something I explain from my own perspective. However, if I truly studied my audience, knew them well, and catered to their perspective, getting everyone to align to my recommended approach or solution was easy.

Many people waste time at work by focusing on what they cannot influence, dwelling on or comparing their work to others, complaining about a company-wide initiative or decision, and discussing obstacles or what they lack in terms of resources and time. Spending energy and effort on these types of things will not change them, so why try? Remember to ask yourself, "Can I influence this?" before giving it the gift of your attention and time. Focus your efforts on the variables you can have an impact on, like getting everyone onboard with a solution, meeting and communication cadences, stakeholder relations, your reputation, and the quality of the work you are assigned to execute. All of these are significant attributes of your work life, and you can influence them. The ability to influence people and outcomes is a highly sought-after skillset that few achieve. The first step to getting there is understanding what you can and cannot influence. Any effort spent toward understanding the reasoning behind something you cannot influence is wasted. It drains you, and nothing comes of it. Be mindful and purposeful on where you spend time and energy. View it as a gift that you provide and use it wisely. Do not use it to over-complicate or critique factors and decisions that you don't own or can't control. If you really want to be seen as valuable and proactively avoid burn out, use your time and effort toward aligning to what you cannot change and influencing what you can. Master the skillsets of asking the right questions, knowing your audience, and getting clear on your objective to become someone who influences outcomes and adds immense value.

Chapter Summary

Lesson	How to Implement	When to Implement
Don't Try to Understand Why If You Can't Influence It	• Recognize that if it's not a fit, it's not a fit—no need to look for deeper meaning • Ask yourself, "Can I influence this?" before putting effort into it • Never care more than your client (the owner or accountable party) • Align your level of effort and buy-in to that of the accountable party • Allow others to make mistakes and own their failures • If you disagree with a variable but cannot influence it, find a way to accept it and move on • Remember that there are multiple paths to successfully meeting an outcome, not just your path • What matters is if you meet your objective • To influence a solution, sell your idea (versus arguing your point) by knowing your audience and asking the right questions	• When you are the responsible party • When you want to affect an outcome • When you are driving a meeting or discussion

Chapter 8

There Is an Art and Science to Everything

Once I had several consulting projects under my belt, I was asked to spend time creating the methodology for a new service my firm wanted to offer called organizational design. My job was to define and create the processes and tools consultants would follow to align a company's structure, job descriptions, processes, technology, and culture with their overall strategy. I worked full-time on creating this methodology for several months. It required a lot of research, interviewing experts, and reviewing existing templates, tools, and processes. Once completed, I trained consultants on the new methodology to ensure everyone leveraged the same approach when executing organizational design work. Afterward, I was staffed on a project that required an expert in this area. I was assigned to work with a group of six individuals who came together to form a new department within their company. One person was a director and the rest were managers. Outside of their assigned titles, these six people had little to no knowledge about how to divvy out responsibilities or even what their full scope of work entailed. I was brought on to draft their organizational chart, job descriptions, and processes. It meant we needed to determine who did what and how, as well as how many additional people they would need to hire to completely staff the new department. I spent my first day educating the team of six on the organizational design methodology. I wanted them to understand there was a proven way to do this work, a scientific approach that we needed to follow and what the path forward looked like. I was excited to ease their anxiety by letting them know there was a "right" way to build a department. We just had to follow the steps outlined in the methodology. Since I had completed months of research studying the scientific approach, I knew the methodology was sound. I knew my skillset and knowledge aligned perfectly to what they were hoping to achieve. *What a perfect fit this project is,* I thought. *They must be so relieved to learn there is a known process we can follow.*

On my second day, the director called me into her office. She said, "While I love the education you've provided, we don't have the luxury of time to complete activities like documenting job descriptions and process mapping. We need to build something that can flex and grow, and we must start doing the work now." I understood what she was saying and agreed because other teams were dependent on hers. Additionally, the executives within the company were looking for her team to immediately perform and demonstrate value. It was expensive to build a new department, and the executives wanted to reap the benefits of their investment as quickly as possible. I told the director I was not sure how we could start executing work without any sort of role description or process in place. She said, "Look, I know you understand the science behind this really well. But there is an art and a science to everything. I'm asking you to figure out the art." I paused to let the words sink in. I thought about it for a moment and then I realized she was right. There was a science and an art to literally everything in the workplace.

I knew that I had to do better. I promised her I would figure out a way and get back to her later in the day. I also realized in that moment that having a solid process in place for how to do something did not always mean everyone would or could follow it. There were other factors to consider outside of what the methodology and research said. I needed to be less rigid and more creative in my thought process, and that was difficult for me. It required me to think outside of the box. I needed to know how to leverage the scientific steps but add a twist that allowed for a flexible solution that fit the unique situation we were in. Even though I was hesitant, I tried. I embraced the ambiguity and told myself there were other ways to be successful. I just had to find one. On my third day, we sat in a room and discussed who would do what and how over the next month. I recorded everything and sent out detailed notes, outlining daily goals for the next 2 weeks. Those six individuals executed that work and moved toward the goals while I drafted processes, organizational charts, and job descriptions based on those notes. I met with each of them individually for 1 hour per week to review drafts and asked what needed to change or how it could be improved. When I had finalized a draft of a process, job description, or organizational chart, I called a meeting. The team came together to review, finalize, and approve it. I published finalized versions to their team site and sent everyone a link. The director hired new people and educated them on responsibilities and expectations based on what we produced. It required multiple versions along the way, and sometimes we scrapped a process or role altogether. We had a lot of quick hallway discussions where I got feedback and had to act fast. We had to share what each role would do, when, and how, in real time. Each day we took blind steps toward progress and moved the department in the right direction. It was not my preferred path to success, but it was the road we had to take in light of the circumstances. In the end, all that really mattered was that it worked.

As that project came to an end and a new one started, I saw time and time again that there was an art and a science to everything I did. The two had a yin-yang relationship and when used simultaneously, offered up the best result. Identifying and balancing the scientific and artistic side of everything was not only applicable to work approaches and solutions, but people too. I noticed that each person I encountered tended to lean toward one or the other. People were either scientists or artists. Most struggled with striking a balance between the two. I already knew I was a scientist. I also knew it meant I needed to be less rigid and more open-minded. I realized it was unrealistic to believe every problem could be solved in a scientific, methodical way and that all I needed to do was find the data or apply the correct process. I needed to dig deep to find the artist within and get creative with my solutions. I had to find new ways of doing things, take risks by trying something that had never been done before, and let go of my desire to plan everything out perfectly before moving forward. I needed to learn how to bring more of the artistic side of myself to the surface in order to add the most value.

One of the best ways I learned about how to bring out the artistic side was to work with and observe people who were artists. I previously avoided collaborating closely with those who were different than me to avoid conflict. Once I grasped that I needed to meld multiple approaches and ways of thinking to get the best result, I developed a deep appreciation for diverse opinions and recommendations.

Stanley was an artist. He felt stifled by methodologies and rules. He did not want to be boxed into something because it suffocated his creativity. He thrived off flexibility, real-time decisions, and loose protocols or guidelines. He wanted to feel free to create something from scratch. Through working with Stanley, I became more comfortable with the idea of having a rough plan in place but knowing we could easily pivot away from that and change course based on new information or circumstances. To become a better artist, I practiced being quick on my feet by doing less planning and practicing before I facilitated a meeting. I also gave myself permission to spend more time dedicated to creative thinking. Stanley told me, "If you're thinking about a solution, you're working." I tested this idea. One Friday, I didn't have any meetings after lunch. I set up a half-day out of office message, shut down my laptop, and left. I spent my afternoon at a park, staring at a sparkling lake and thinking through every angle of a problem my client needed to solve. Stanley's advice was true. When I walked away from that park, I had a solution. I learned that clearing my mind and schedule to think about how to resolve something in a different way was a key piece to the creative process many artists thrived from. It was like meditating on the problem. I only allowed that business problem and the different perspectives of it to cross my mind. I pushed everything else out. As I allowed my thoughts to flow freely past me regarding the problem, thoughts about the solution began to appear, first in pieces and then more holistically. I slowly shifted my focus from the problem to each aspect of the solution until I knew how to glue it all together and could articulate my recommendation for how to solve it.

Another way I strengthened the artistic side of my approach was by facilitating workshops with my clients. I initially was asked to do this, but over time began to volunteer. It was a great way to flex my artistic brain muscle. I never knew which activities or discussions would land best with which participants, so I had to be quick to read their non-verbal feedback and pivot to a different activity or pose a different question in order to keep their attention and focus. The artistic side was less structured and had fewer rules. There was room for more complex, gray areas. Artists liked the gray area because it allowed for different interpretations. It gave them permission to try new things that had never been done before. As I developed my artistic side, I realized the artistic and scientific sides were equally important. Moreover, the two complemented one another. I still needed to be a scientist and learn what the proven methodology was to get from point A to point B. I naturally gravitated toward a mindset that simplified problems by making them black and white. But I also needed to be an artist and think about the context and circumstances specific to the issue I was dealing with, like the culture of the client company, the stakeholder impacts and personalities, and what had and had not worked in the past. I used that information to infuse my own artistic flavor into the scientific solution I was implementing. Infusing the two also required me to step back and see the bigger picture. I avoided getting bogged down by details and rules, which allowed me to identify the best solution.

In order to embrace the scientific side of the solution, I first had to acknowledge the proven method. That was known as the methodology, and there was always at least one. Whether it was the methodology for how to manage a re-org or restructuring, how to kick-off a new initiative, how to implement a new process or software system, how to stand up a new policy, or how to measure a team's success, it was always there. I just had to find it. It required research and identifying and talking to SMEs. The scientific side of the approach always came first. I had to first educate myself on what the methodology and data said about how to get from the current to the future, or desired, state. I also needed to understand and build an awareness of the business norms and rules. This was easy for me because I enjoyed and even thrived off guidelines and structure. For Stanley and most artists, an obstacle to abiding by or trying a scientific approach was accepting rules. For artists, rules were something that stifled creativity.

I had a professor in graduate school who used to say, "Remember the rules were meant to be bent, not broken," when describing how to navigate our way through corporate landscapes. She told us that in our quest to achieve the best result, we would encounter many hurdles, some of which were in the form of a business rule. She said sometimes the best way to leap over that hurdle was to find a way around the rule, to bend it slightly so we could still achieve the best result within the guidelines. I never wanted to fully break a business rule or corporate standard because that could lead to disaster. However, there were several times in my career when I ran into a rule or norm that was the only thing standing between the problem and the solution. In those moments, I found it necessary to bend the rules. One example is when I worked for a company who despised PowerPoint. I was told not to use it, to stick to spreadsheets and documents. However, after working there for about a year, I was asked to create a roadmap for a solution, and I knew the best tool to present that in was PowerPoint. I needed to show a timeline, milestones, inputs, and outputs. There were other tools I could have used, but the only options available to me were PowerPoint, Word, and Excel. I bent the rule and built my roadmap using a slide. I didn't ask permission; I needed to land the solution and knew a visual was required to do so. I presented my slide to the client and a few stakeholders in a meeting. I began the meeting by stating that I understood this was not the ideal format, but it was the best tool to build a visual that could quickly and easily land all of the complexities of the solution. I informed them that once we had approval for the high-level map, we would use other tools to share the information broadly. The team never pushed back. They reviewed it, agreed the format was necessary, and shared my slide broadly. They called out the caveat that it was an exception to the rule, but as it turned out, the rule needed to be bent and nobody really cared because it was less important to them than the solution I was presenting.

I was reminded of this advice about bending but not breaking rules when I looked to strike the balance between an artist and a scientist. Scientists should be more flexible about rules. Artists should acknowledge and learn the rules and remember not to go so far as to break them. An artist does not necessarily have to color inside the lines, but they should know where the lines are. Stanley viewed rules as guardrails on a long, windy road. He stayed inside the guardrails, even though he often brushed up against them going 75mph. Rules and norms served a purpose, so they were important to understand and be aware of. The other piece that artists needed to accept was that learning the methodology did not mean he had to follow it exactly.

It just meant there was an awareness and understanding of the best practice. The science side and methodology needed to be learned and leveraged. The proven process and data served as the solution's foundation. Rules associated with the organization and context surrounding team norms, history, and culture also needed to be known. Once they were, the solution needed to be saturated with the artistic side – innovative ideas, flexibility, and open-mindedness. That was how to identify the best solution possible for any organizational problem.

In order to embrace working with and learning from those who differed from my own style, I first needed to be able to identify others' communication and workstyle preferences. I knew that in the workplace setting, we each liked things done a certain way. Each person had their own personal style that they viewed as the most advantageous way to complete work. Preferences ranged in terms of working within teams versus autonomously, how information was conveyed and presented, and how timelines, deliverables, and approaches to solving a problem were identified. Workstyle preferences did not necessarily align to personal lifestyle preferences. For example, many people, like myself, were extroverts in their personal life and introverts in their work life. I gained energy from social interaction with friends and family, but at work, I preferred to complete my tasks independently. It drained me to collaborate.

Recognizing my own preferences as well as those of the people around me was a powerful tool that served me well in terms of influencing others, building my brand, and maintaining professional boundaries. It was something I became knowledgeable about over the course of a few years by reading and taking self-assessments. Many companies I worked with also offered workstyle assessments during corporate retreats, conferences, trainings, new employee orientations, all-hands meetings, or something similar. I also found and took portions of assessments online for free. There were many to choose from and the characteristics each described regarding communication and workstyle preferences also varied. Because of the wide variety of assessments and categorization of preferred styles, it was difficult to remember, especially when most assessments detailed three to five attributes per person. I could not easily remember several attributes and categorizations across the multiple colleagues and stakeholders I interacted with. I set out to simplify it and over time developed a quick and easy way to remember workstyle preferences. Once I identified which workstyle preference someone had, I adjusted my approach to them accordingly. I simplified the need to memorize multiple attributes about each person by placing them into one of two buckets: people-oriented or task-oriented. I observed others and asked myself a few questions about their behavior to determine which bucket they should be placed in. Observations included whether they wanted or needed to have a conversation before diving into work objectives, whether they regularly took breaks to chat with others, and if they enjoyed personal stories or random hallway discussions. If the answer to all or most of these questions was yes, I placed that person in the people-oriented bucket. If said person instead preferred to jump into details of work during a conversation, seemed stressed, uncomfortable, or checked out during hallway discussions, or consistently checked the time during small talk at the beginning or end of a meeting, then I placed that person in the task-oriented bucket.

By placing my client, stakeholders, leaders, and colleagues into one of these two buckets, I was able to easily adjust my approach to fit their workstyle with minimal effort. If the person was people-oriented, I started every conversation by asking, "How are you today?" I gave them a few minutes to get the personal connection going before diving into work objectives. For the task-oriented person, I approached them by immediately sharing the reason or objective for my interruption of their time. Task-oriented people, like myself, needed to know what would be achieved by stopping progress in one area to focus on another. Interruptions for questions or conversations was not how they wanted to spend their time, so I needed to make it clear why my interruption for a question or to get an opinion was a good use of their time. I directed the conversation toward objectives with people-oriented workstyles and allowed those with task-oriented workstyles to direct the conversation once they knew my primary objective for meeting with them. By making this subtle adjustment based on who I was interacting with, I found that my meetings and conversations were much more productive, and my work relationships improved. To my surprise, I even sensed an unspoken appreciation for my extra effort. I quickly realized that task and people orientations were also indicative of an artistic or scientific preferred approach. Not surprisingly, a person with a task orientation was typically a scientist. A good conversation could go a long way for an artist, especially with someone they respected. Bouncing ideas off others was a great way to brainstorm better solutions.

Recognizing the correlation between people and task-oriented styles to artists and scientists gave me insight into how people thought about and approached solutions. If I recognized someone as task-oriented, I realized they often viewed solutions from a scientific standpoint. That meant I needed to infuse more of the artistic, creative element by pushing for us to think outside the box or bringing up specific circumstances that meant we needed to consider other factors in our process. This ensured our approach was well-rounded. Likewise, someone who I identified as people-oriented often needed reminders of the guardrails, or rules, and while I was happy to serve as the person the artist bounced ideas off of, I also sought to educate him or her on proven methodologies and theories that had worked in similar situations and environments. Tying workstyle preferences to how a person thought about and approached work was revolutionary for me. It allowed me to adjust my approach, so I was first respected and heard by others, and then able to provide new ways of thinking that added value to our overall goal, approach, decision, or solution.

Your job will require you to wear the hat of both a scientist and an artist. In addition, understanding that people are either artists or scientists and building the skillset to tap into whichever one is needed based on the audience helps you get ahead. Remember scientists prefer structure and methodology. Black and white. Fact or fiction. The benefit of the scientific side of a solution is that it is simplified, proven to work, and provides a process and rules to follow for how to achieve your goal. While not all artists are people-oriented, many are. Artists are full of creative solutions; they are the big idea people. The best way to come up with ideas and evolve them into an original, powerful solution is by brainstorming with others. The benefit of the artistic side of a solution is that it is new and exciting. It brings an energy of enthusiasm that often motivates people. When the scientific and artistic mindset are combined, it is inevitable that the best possible solution will emerge. Learn how to infuse both flavors into your thinking, approach, and solutions. Learn to appreciate each and take a step back to ask yourself if each area is well-represented in your recommendations and approach to problem-solving. When working with others, identify their preferred workstyle and look for how that is represented in the ideas and approaches they recommend. Adjust your feedback and collaboration style accordingly. Most importantly, recognize that even when you cannot see it, there is a science and art in everything you do. Take steps toward becoming a master in both areas. The ability to do so is rare and enables you to bring more robust solutions to the table.

Chapter Summary

Lesson	How to Implement	When to Implement
There is an Art and Science to Everything	• Be a scientist: learn the methodology, know the rules, understand guardrails • Be an artist: see the big picture, create, think outside the box • Acknowledge that time spent thinking about business problems is time spent working • Remember rules were meant to be bent not broken • Break down business problems from the perspective of both artist and scientist • Identify if people are task-oriented or people-oriented by observing how often they converse and begin a conversation • When starting a conversation, ask people-oriented folks how they are doing; tell task-oriented folks the objective of the conversation first • Embrace differing workstyles and mindsets, view it as one of the best ways to learn, and evolve your approach	• When identifying or discussing a solution • When interacting or collaborating with others

Chapter 9

This Is What You Do, Not Who You Are

A few years into my career as a management consultant, Jill left our firm. During her tenure there, she married and had two children. Her husband's job took them an hour north of Seattle, and she was commuting daily. The commute and ability to strike a balance between work and home life became increasingly difficult for her. She took a new job that was closer to home and offered her more consistency and flexibility. Even with our hectic schedules, we kept in touch. One day, a couple of years after she left, we met for lunch. Jill told me she was on the hunt for a job yet again. She said her company had restructured, and she was placed on a new team. The manager of that team had a different expectation than the manager who hired her, and it was no longer the right fit. I asked her how the interview process was going. She told me that in her pursuit of a new job, she wanted to ensure it was the right fit and was telling interviewers, "My job is very important to me, but it is what I do, not who I am." While I agreed that work-life balance was valuable, my initial reaction to that phrase was that it seemed a bit harsh. I interpreted it as something that would discourage potential employers from hiring her or make for a bad first impression. I asked her how the interviewers were responding. She told me the reaction was mixed based on facial expressions, but that was not her concern. She said those who understood and related were the ones she wanted to work with and for.

A few years later, I also left the company Jill and I worked for. I joined a different consulting firm that did not require me to travel and expanded the list of client companies I could add to my resume. Jill's words stayed with me as I realized more and more the importance of differentiating between what you do and who you are. Few people recognize that there is tremendous value in achieving work-life balance, or as I refer to it, work-life health. It wasn't always possible to maintain a 50-50 balance, but it was possible to ensure my work life had healthy boundaries and I did not allow it to take over my personal life. I saw what happened when work life was no longer healthy, and became the only type of life someone had. Many of my colleagues, clients, and stakeholders worked around the clock. They were expecting to finally catch up and then have more free time, only to find that there was always more to do. While their intentions were in the right place, what they were trying to achieve – a moment where they had crossed everything off their to do lists – never occurred. Even worse, all the extra hours were often at the expense of their own sanity and health.

I had a mentor tell me once, "90 percent of what you do at work will be forgotten." I initially took offense to that comment. I interpreted it as a critique of the work I was doing, that it meant either the work I was assigned was not important or what I produced was not high quality. I asked her to clarify, and she went on to explain that most of the work we do must be re-done at some point because of external influences, such as the economy or customer demand, or internal changes to the organization, such as a new structure, strategy, or leaders. Our work became outdated, the company decided to go a different route, someone down the line dropped the ball, the project lost momentum, or a myriad of other reasons. But in the end, the fact was most of what we did wouldn't last and would be forgotten years or, in some cases, months later. I viewed this advice as a business rule and remembered it throughout each project I was assigned. It helped put my work life into perspective. When I found myself distressed about someone's lack of participation or my own desire for perfection, I would think, *how much will this matter a couple years from now?* My answer, almost always, was that it wouldn't matter. We were doing business on a global scale in a fast-paced, technology-driven environment, and everything was re-evaluated, re-prioritized and re-purposed constantly. Remembering that most of what I did would be forgotten helped me prioritize my personal life. That was where I had the potential to have a greater, long-standing impact on my family, my friends, and the life I was building for myself.

Reminding myself that most of what I did would be forgotten could've been an easy excuse for me not to care about my work or feel passionate about adding value and doing my best. My colleague said the other side to this rule was that I had to do the 90 percent that did not matter in order to get to the 10 percent that did. I had to put in the time and effort because what I was doing mattered in that moment of time, but I needed to recognize when I was working on something that fell in that 90 percent versus that 10 percent. If I was caught up on something that fell in that 90 percent, then there was no reason to agonize or be a perfectionist. The task I was completing was simply a means to an end. The time to revise and bring out the perfectionist side was when we got through the trenches and came out the other side to complete the final deliverable, or the 10 percent, that would have a lasting impact. I knew that pushing myself too hard in that 90 percent phase was not going to serve me well in the long run. It also did not serve me well to not put any effort into that 90 percent phase or try to find ways to avoid it altogether. There were a lot of people I interacted with who did the minimum requirement to get by. They were disliked by many of my stakeholders, had a poor reputation, and seldom moved up in the organization. I did not want to tarnish my brand by not showing up or being present when I was working. But by following this rule, I learned it was equally important not to tarnish it by working around the clock. If I had, I would not have been able to think clearly and efficiently, and that meant I could not produce good work.

Following the "90 percent of your work will be forgotten but is necessary to get to the 10 percent that matters" rule shifted my perspective on how to achieve work-life health. Another piece of advice that further shifted my perspective was, "You teach people how to treat you." I had heard the phrase before, as it was popularized through many topical discussion television shows and mainstream media, but it was not until a colleague mentioned it in the context of work that I realized how necessary it was to apply the message to work-life health goals. Understanding that the way colleagues, clients, stakeholders, and managers treated me was based on their interpretation of my verbal and non-verbal cues heightened my awareness of the expectations I was setting. In my experience, most people were highly motivated when beginning a new job or role. They wanted to prove their competence and validate the decision to hire them as quickly as possible. They volunteered to take on more and worked long hours to demonstrate their commitment and dedication. What they seemed to be unaware of was that their approach set the wrong tone for the long-term. It told their colleagues and leaders where the bar should be. They unintentionally communicated that they were available to take on more and willing to work long hours.

In the era of advanced technology, we are always connected. People can send me emails, texts, instant messages, or call my cell phone outside of typical work hours, and they often did initially. I knew I had to teach them how to treat me. I had to draw the boundaries for them. The best way for me to do this in terms of how and when I communicated was through non-verbal signals. I had a hard rule that I did not respond to any emails (unless it was truly urgent) outside of the hours of 7am to 6pm. That did not necessarily mean I was not working outside of those hours. There were times when work was busier than usual, and I needed to temporarily put in long hours. However, I still followed my 7am to 6pm rule. If I broke that rule, then I would be teaching the sender that it was okay to contact me after hours and that he or she should expect a response. That was not what I wanted the expectation to be. Sometimes I had so many emails in my inbox that I needed to read and draft responses outside of work hours, but that was all I did. I drafted the emails and saved them. The next morning, at 7am, I opened my saved emails, proofread each, and hit send. Did it really have a negative impact if I sent an email at 7am instead of 9pm the night before? What I realized by following this rule was that sending emails late at night did not have a negative effect on the company, only on me. I also knew they were getting a much better, well thought out response, because I allowed myself time to digest and reply. I even circled back and proofread after a night of rest, which often allowed me to improve my email responses even more, because I was coming back to the communication with fresh eyes and a clear mindset.

In terms of how quickly I responded, Stanley taught me to follow a 48-hour rule. I applied it to myself and others. I gave people 2 full days to respond to a message I sent and reached out on the third day with a reminder if I had not heard from them. People seemed in agreement with that timeframe, like they genuinely appreciated my follow-up a few days later. Less than 48 hours was pushy, and longer than that conveyed the non-verbal message that my ask was not important. I also gave myself 48 hours to respond to an email. That meant if I did not know how to respond to something in the moment, I had the time and space to think through it, which allowed me to form a clear, articulate, and appropriate response. The 48-hour rule was especially helpful for emails that expressed frustration, were confusing, or caught me off guard. There were times when I received an urgent email that required an immediate response. However, it was quite obvious when this was the case, and it almost always occurred during working hours. While it depends on the role you play within an organization, for me, the sender really could not expect a response to an urgent email at 10pm. There was no way to report that as non-compliant or a major miss when the urgency happened way outside of agreed upon working hours. As long as I responded right away in the morning, it was considered a quick response because my boundaries were already set. It was also so rare that it didn't have an impact on my work-life health.

I also didn't respond when I took time off. I needed my employer and stakeholders to know that when I was out of office, they needed to respect my time. I was afraid to do this at first, particularly early on in my career. I didn't want to be interpreted as a slacker or lazy, but I took the advice of my colleague and forced myself to follow this rule. To my delight, it worked even better than I expected. I initially anticipated judgment and that others would express concern to my manager or client. I was shocked when the opposite happened. Over time, they stopped emailing and texting me after hours and during vacation. They learned to expect that they would not receive a response and they stopped trying. The best part was that, more times than not, they followed suit. Those I worked closest with started to shut down on vacation and rarely sent emails after hours.

An example I observed of people neglecting to follow the "you teach people how to treat you" advice came in the form of volunteering their time or opinions. People chimed in during a large meeting with their two cents regarding how something should be done without being prompted. If they wanted to impress a leader, they would volunteer to do something they didn't really know how to do. This was especially true for new hires. I sat in many a meeting where a new hire came onboard and stated they could own creating a process or write up a policy because they had done it in previous roles for other companies. However, they neglected to factor in their lack of experience and understanding of the details behind how the company operated. That meant they didn't understand all the ins-and-outs of how other processes, roles, or teams would be impacted. They often had to revise their work and set up several meetings for input, review, and approval. Other times, there was a standing report or deliverable under review, and someone said they could make it better by adding new data and graphs or visuals. When they went to improve it, they realized that the only information that was available was already included. In order to build the report or deliverable out with additional data points, they had to set up a process to collect and enter it into a system. Then, they had to identify how to analyze and format it. Again, they didn't have all the information before volunteering. Furthermore, they were inserting themselves in places that were not part of their primary responsibilities. The result was they were then expected to own more when they didn't have the bandwidth or knowledge to do so. While I appreciated their desire to be helpful, it was clear their approach was not well thought out. They needed to be diligent and intentional with how they offered their help. The right way was either to ask the owner if they had considered certain aspects of a problem or to state a recommendation and provide the reasoning. That was something that could be done in a one-on-one conversation. However, what I saw was people stating their opinions in a group setting while, intentionally or unintentionally, positioning themselves as an expert and their opinions as factual. These same people were then surprised when they were asked to own something or viewed as the SME.

Sometimes, their behavior seemed to be egocentric. It was a desire to impress leadership by speaking in a meeting, and then being taken aback by the unintended consequence – a "fake it until you make it" attempt gone wrong. Other times, I thought the person was genuinely trying to help, but they cared too much. They cared more than the owner and could not find peace in letting the owner of the work fail. Sometimes teaching people how to treat you means letting others fail. It made sense to state a recommendation or opinion on improvement if someone had concerns about the direction of the work. However, people who fought for it to be done their way taught everyone else that they wanted to take on more responsibility. Then those people would find themselves working around the clock because they couldn't let others own their mistakes.

You teach people how to treat you in everything you do. When someone is tired or stressed and then speaks angrily or with frustration to their co-workers, they reciprocate because the unspoken message conveyed is that there's no respect for one another, and it's therefore okay to be rude. Or worse, the person on the receiving end of the anger retaliates by refusing to collaborate or follow through with anything from that point on. I realized the advice "you teach people how to treat you" and finding work-life health were intertwined and had a cyclical relationship. It was much easier to show people how to treat me when I was experiencing work-life health because I was well-rested and clear-minded. If I was overwhelmed and burned out, then I didn't have the patience and wherewithal to be at the top of my game and successfully teach people how to treat me. Likewise, if I didn't set expectations and give non-verbal cues on how I needed to be treated, it was significantly more difficult to achieve work-life balance. To be effective, I clung to Jill's words and told myself work was only what I did. My career did not solely define who I was, so I never let it.

Part of teaching people how to treat me meant I had to learn to put less weight on what others thought. Jill shared a story with me once that helped me to recognize and digest the power behind this shift. She told me she was staffed on a project that required her to put in a lot of extra hours. She was part of a large team, made up of 50+ people who were implementing a new software system. She and a colleague were working on some training material for the upcoming implementation. Jill said she checked her watch and suddenly realized it was almost 4pm. Her son was in a play at 5:30 that evening and since she lived an hour's drive north, she needed to rush out the door in order to make it on time. She told her colleague she had to run. Jill said the colleague shot her a look of disbelief and rolled her eyes. Jill told her that she could stay if she needed to; her colleague gave her a frustrated look and shrugged. Jill felt guilty and called her husband to let him know she would miss the play. She later told me that was one of her biggest regrets. The training material was not needed for another couple of days, and she missed her son's first play. I began to critique her colleague in the story when she interrupted me and said, "It's not her fault." I must have looked puzzled because she continued: "It was my fault for caring too much what she thought of me." While most people took my non-verbal cues and respected my time away from work, there were a few who expected something different. They were the people who worked around the clock and did not value work-life health. Their expectation was that because they chose to put in extra hours outside of work, everyone else needed to as well. I realized that their opinions didn't matter to me because they were not the type of people I respected and admired. More importantly, they were not who I wanted to make decisions on what was best for me and how I spent my time. That was a privilege only I could own. Giving my colleagues the power to influence my decisions about how to divide work and personal time would be foolish and self-destructive.

One key skillset I had to learn in order to leave work at work was how to prioritize. The way prioritization was defined for me by Jill was knowing when to give an A+ versus a C+. This traced back to understanding that some of the work I did would be forgotten or sit on a shelf. I needed to ask myself what the priority of the client or leader was. I needed to know what on my plate had the most visibility and dependencies. With each new task I was assigned, I repeatedly asked myself, "Is this a must-have or a nice-to-have?" I gave the "must-haves" my A-game, divvied out my B-level effort to the "somewhere in between," and gave my C-level effort to the "nice-to-haves."

Nothing ever got less than a C, but it was unrealistic to think everything could get an A+ and I would still have time for a personal life. There were times when it felt like everything required an A+ effort. In those moments I first had to ask myself if I was putting too much pressure on myself or if everything on my plate truly impacted several people, was something my client was prioritizing, or had a high level of visibility with leadership. At times, but rarely, it was true that everything needed an A+, and that meant I needed to approach my manager or client overseeing the work. I would schedule a meeting with him or her and say, "I have these four things on my plate right now. I can't get to all of them. I can either give some of this my A+ effort and some of it my C+ effort, or I can give two things my A+ effort and do the other two later or give them to someone else. How would you prefer to move forward?" I had to be able to speak to how much time was spent on each initiative and why, but the response was always positive. I was never questioned or viewed as a slacker. What was important was that I truly couldn't get everything done, and that was clear. If that was unclear, I gave the client or manager in-depth insight into how I spent my time on each piece of work and the number of hours each task was taking or would take. I learned how to speak about being overwhelmed due to owning more work than I could complete by practicing. In addition, I told the client or leader as early on as possible. Since the client was the accountable person and owner in the scenario, that meant it was their job to guide me on prioritization. If I was unsure what was most and least important, then the next logical step was to ask. What I found astonishing was that the more I tried to achieve work-life health by prioritizing, teaching people how to treat me, and setting boundaries, the more I realized the fear that I would be viewed in a negative light was unfounded and only existed in my head.

My conversation with the manager or client regarding

how to prioritize my work was one in which I was asking for feedback, but I was also setting clear boundaries. I learned this was something I had to do continually. It was important to define expectations upfront when I started a new project. I defined my role and scope, when I would be available, meetings I was expected to attend, and the overall business objective with my client. What I learned was that my client would require a reminder of the expectations we set somewhat regularly. Not to say that I was unable to join a meeting last minute or be flexible when new information arose, and we had to pivot our direction – I could be agile, but it was vital to define some general boundaries and hold my client accountable to them. One instance was informing my client I would work remotely on Fridays. I told every client that on my first day. That was one way I could get more work done and avoid full days of meetings every day. A few weeks later, I would inevitably be asked where I was on Friday. I reminded them of my boundary. I didn't offer an explanation. Jill taught me that when people ask a question in the workplace, they typically want a quick response, not the entire back story and four paragraphs on the reasoning behind something. In fact, an explanation was rarely required and shouldn't be proactively offered, but rather, only shared when requested. I found that when I said, "I work remotely on Fridays," the client typically replied with something like, "Oh yes, I forgot. Thank you" or "My mistake" and then asked their question via instant message or email.

My initial instinct had been to explain why or offer to come in if they needed me. After Jill's advice, I fought that instinct and instead waited for them to ask. I was delighted to learn that 99 percent of the time, they didn't require a deeper explanation. I also realized that people often proactively sign themselves up for a due date or offer explanations unnecessarily. As they offer the explanation, they try to address the assumed reason for why someone is asking by offering to do more or go above and beyond. This always leads to the same outcome: an imbalance between work and life, tipping the scales toward undesired overtime and, in some cases, an inability to follow through. Many times, I was asked to take on something new and different that was vaguely related to my work but not within the scope of my responsibilities. In those moments, I had to have the type of difficult conversation that no one wants to have because it makes people uncomfortable. I would remind myself, "This is just a job" to get rid of unnecessary angst and tell my client that what they were requesting was not in scope. I told them that I wanted to be as helpful as possible, but that I couldn't realistically take on a new book of work in addition to my current scope and still do a good job. I always offered alternate solutions, like asking my firm for another consultant, or if I could, help when my current scope was completed, but I never said yes. I knew it was better to say no than to say yes and not follow through. That knowledge became key to my ability to shift away from being a people pleaser who gave an enthusiastic yes to new requests so people would like me. I interacted with many people who said yes to everything that was asked of them. I worked with them or alongside them and saw time and time again they just couldn't meet their commitments. People said yes to please their boss or a senior leader without realizing what they were taking on. Once they understood the weight of what they had taken on, they tried to back pedal, or worse, opted to avoid the problem altogether, became difficult to track down, and then slowly stopped returning emails or phone calls. They couldn't follow through and they panicked. It ruined their reputation, as they were then viewed as unreliable and untrustworthy. Sometimes the consequences were even more palpable, such as monetary deductions or a write-up in their personnel folder, all because they didn't know how to say no and set healthy boundaries.

Unless you have recently founded your own business or joined a start-up that requires you to work around the clock, your job is what you do, not who you are. Who you are is, and should be, multi-faceted. You have a lot of titles. Some of them may include parent, partner, spouse, friend, child, sibling, chef, author, gardener, artist, musician, avid reader, fitness guru, movie buff, and the list goes on. Don't get so tied up in your title at work that it's the only thing you make time for. Give quality time to your other titles and roles as well. It will help you keep a healthy emotional distance from work and maintain balance in your life. It will allow you to put yourself in a mindset where you can be more efficient and productive at work because it is not the only thing you do all the time. Allow yourself to check in and out of work each day. Allow yourself to set boundaries, say no, and unplug after hours. Prioritize yourself, and you will find that time spent at work is more exhilarating and focused. You will also start to care less about what others think and more about what you think, and that is a mindset worth achieving.

Chapter Summary

Lesson	How to Implement	When to Implement
This is What You Do, Not Who You Are	• Prioritize work-life balance • Remember 90% of what you do will be forgotten, but you must do the 90% to get to the 10% that matters • Act from the perspective that you teach people how to treat you • Set rules for email communication, such as only responding during certain hours, and giving yourself and others 48 hours to reply • Know when to give an A+ versus a C+ • Remind yourself it is just a job • Set expectations over and over and over • Recognize that it is better to say no than to say yes and not follow through	• Communication after hours or while out of the office • When working with your supervisor to define the scope of your role • When completing a deliverable or launching an initiative • When interacting with a team or group of people

Chapter 10

Take Inventory

One best practice I was told about early on in my career was the importance of facilitating a project "postmortem" at the end of every initiative I worked on. I would invite all of the team members who helped successfully land or launch the initiative to reflect back on the life of the project and identify what lessons were learned. If we did it all over again, what would we do the same, and what would we do differently? We would summarize best practices so that groups who worked on similar initiatives in the future could leverage our learnings. We talked through roles, tools, templates, meeting cadences – every aspect of our work.

Well into my tenure as a management consultant, I realized I could apply this technique of reflecting on the past and incorporating learnings for my own career path. I scheduled regular check-ins with myself to take self-inventory. I asked myself if I still felt my career was the right fit. I thought about everything I had learned, what skills I still wanted to master, and what my next steps and future career goals were. I put time aside once every 3 to 6 months for self-inventory. I would block my calendar for a half-day on a Friday. If I could, I would not be in the office. If I had to be in the office on self-inventory day, I booked a conference room or asked to borrow someone's office (as a consultant, I never had an office) where I could be hidden away and have quiet time to think. It was my time to reset, and I felt no guilt scheduling it during working hours. The truth was that this practice served me and my company well. If I determined I wanted to stay, that reiterated my commitment to the company and the work I was assigned. If I determined it was time to go, then I was saving the company from having a disgruntled employee who no longer desired to be there and because of that wouldn't be as beneficial to them.

I started by reflecting on the past. I visualized where I had been and how far I had come. All the different projects, stakeholder meetings, client conversations, and key teaching moments with mentors surfaced to the top of my memory. It reminded me what I learned through my failures and successes. I felt grateful for all the tools and knowledge I had acquired. I felt humbled and proud realizing how far I had come since my first day. After I reflected on my past, I would shift my thoughts to reflect on the present. I would remind myself that whatever was plaguing me was temporary. I closed my eyes and visualized a thick black line, about 2 feet long. I thought of it as my career timeline. I reminded myself that a tiny section of it, maybe 1 centimeter of that 1-foot line, represented the present. Whatever problem I was experiencing was a quick blip on the radar, and it would soon become part of my history. I would add it to the list of memories I could feel proud of – memories of moments I overcame obstacles and chose growth over stagnation.

It was easy to get caught up in present day problems and frustrations. Adding the practice of taking self-inventory into my routine helped remind me that present day pain was temporary and meant I was still growing. As I visualized that 2-foot line, I would think about the future of my career and focus on the portion of the line, or continuum, that represented the unknown. What new advice, tools, relationships, and information would I acquire? How would it help shape my career? How would it help me progress? Since most of the time what I was doing was the right fit for me, thinking about my future career endeavors brought feelings of excitement. If I felt anger or sadness when reflecting on my path, then it would be a sign that it was time to make an adjustment and possibly pick a new career. I turned my attention toward the skillsets and goals I wanted to achieve. I wrote down two or three goals I wanted to accomplish over the next 1 to 5 years. I reflected on whether or not the company I was with was the place to achieve my goals. Writing down goals and committing to them kept me focused and motivated. It enabled me to continue on my career path and face whatever learning curve I was going through with courage and determination. Thinking about the future and identifying new goals provided me with direction. I was moving toward something. Writing it down forced me to clearly define my ideal path, and made my goals measurable. Taking self-inventory kept me centered and focused. It helped me avoid pitfalls, like getting caught up in the chaos of whatever I was currently working on. It also empowered me because it was my opportunity to determine my future. I could decide if I needed to change my career path or employer to better align myself to my goals, objectives, passions, and intentions. I chose how I wanted to refine and grow both myself and my career path.

Over time, my practice evolved, and it was not only self-inventory that I took. The idea of taking inventory applied to many aspects of my career. Another way to interpret the concept was to take inventory of the intellectual property I produced and acquired. I saved everything I created, including the lessons I acquired on each project, and added them to my toolkit inventory. I organized collateral, such as deliverables, presentations, and advice, by topic or project name. Sometimes I revisited my repository when I took self-inventory to get a tangible sense of all the learning I acquired. Most of the time I reviewed my inventory when I needed to re-use a template, review previous research I conducted, or remind myself of a process or approach I used because it applied to my current situation. As my career progressed, I built up my toolkit to include many templates and tools that were applicable to a variety of companies, projects, problems, and circumstances throughout my career. It helped me avoid reinventing the wheel, which added to my ability to achieve work-life health. Inventorying my toolkit and knowledge was a way to consistently apply methodologies and processes that had previously been successful to a new and different set of problems and stakeholders. I still had to transform the tool, template, or knowledge to fit the current situation, but it was easier than starting from scratch. It also further defined my brand because it developed into a unique personal touch that I brought to each new company and project.

The word inventory was first introduced to me through the self-assessments I took to score my communication preferences and workstyles. These assessments often included the word inventory in the name. I also had several projects where I gained exposure to inventory systems and supply chain processes. I realized it was a polysemic word, and looked it up one day. According to Merriam-Webster, the definition of inventory is trifold. The first way is the classic definition, "an itemized list of current assets." I viewed this as my toolkit inventory that housed all of my knowledge and templates. The private company data contained in a template was my client's asset, not mine. However, anything I created and scrubbed free of company data, such as an outline of a presentation or document, formulas I had set up to create a spreadsheet that auto-calculated information, or a communication template outline that described the primary purpose of each paragraph, was mine. Those templates could be revisited and leveraged as needed later on. I also kept the materials from conferences and professional trainings. The valuable advice I received and documented throughout my career rounded out the list of assets I had acquired. I did my best to keep these items organized and cataloged so they were easily accessible. I worked hard to add to my list of assets. I knew that the more I had, the more valuable of a resource I was to a company or team. When I struggled through a problem or project, thinking about the assets I acquired and would continue to gain served as motivation to push myself through.

The second way Merriam-Webster defines inventory is

as "a survey of natural resources." I was less familiar with this interpretation but realized it was a type of inventory I was already taking. I viewed it as the free resources that surrounded me at work. On my first day at each client site, I would walk around the building, surveying the layout. I found the supply room, copy room, conference rooms, and kitchen. I took note of what was available so I could plan to take lunches or use the cafeteria, be aware of what office supplies were on hand, know how to print and make copies, and note which types of conference rooms worked best for one-on-one meetings versus a workshop or training. I also went to the company's intranet and reviewed any tools they had available. Some companies had dictionaries so I could learn their language while others had organizational charts so I could learn names and faces. All had articles and newsletters posted regarding what was trending in the company, information about new product releases, and guidance for new hires. I familiarized myself with all the available resources so I could utilize them to their fullest potential. Knowing what resources were available played a vital role in defining the approach I used to complete my research at the beginning of a new initiative. I often needed to understand a methodology or emulate a process that some other group had already implemented in a different department. I used existing company knowledge, like a public SharePoint or alternate document repository, where I could search for project postmortems and lessons learned. Viewing the internet as a free resource helped me tremendously in the brainstorming process. I watched free videos to learn how to perform a task, like building complex animations into a presentation. I asked my client and stakeholders about other groups who had done what we were trying to do and looked them up using the company directory. I wanted to leverage the knowledge of those people and collect their thoughts prior to launching our initiative.

A lot of consultants and employees say they don't have the resources they need to be successful. They think they need access to advanced research databases with the latest business trends, a person who can train them on how to perform advanced Excel functions, or a sophisticated dashboard outlining several metrics. While these things help, there are always ways to be successful without them. Those who can't see that lack an awareness of this inventory. They miss out on the endless free resources surrounding us, which are key to doing more with less.

The third definition of inventory from Merriam-Webster was also a familiar one: "a list of traits, preferences, attitudes, interests, or abilities used to evaluate personal characteristics or skills." That definition aligned to the way I had first recognized the term inventory. It spoke to what I thought of as relational inventories, such as skillsets, workstyles, and communication preferences. To be effective, I had to inventory the preferences, traits, characteristics, and skillsets of those who I worked for and with. I also had to be aware of my own and how that affected my perception of others, and their perception of me. I needed to look for and be aware of how I was being perceived by others. Questions like, "How are people reacting to me?" and "Where and how can I improve?" were essential for furthering my ability to work more effectively with others.

Ignoring these cues from colleagues and stakeholders manifested itself in the form of self-*un*awareness. I chose to put effort into adjusting my preferred communication or workstyle so I could be better understood and heard by those who were different to me. I started to learn about how I was perceived, what my preferences were, and how they differed from others by taking the time to complete these inventories. Taking personal inventory also meant listening to and asking for feedback from my colleagues, customers, direct reports, and leadership. Sometimes I had to ask for it, but many times it was provided without being requested. I picked up on facial expressions when I spoke and other non-verbal cues that signaled if people agreed with me, seemed hesitant, or were disinterested. I searched for feedback via tone of voice, interruptions, or sudden change of topics. If I experienced any of those, it meant I had lost my audience. It was important to keep them engaged. I learned that feedback via recognition of reactions during interactions was often more honest and useful than when I made a direct request for it.

I built my relational inventory by taking note of others' skillsets and preferences. One of the benefits was it enabled me to identify who was the SME in what area and leverage their expertise to build my own knowledge. Another perk was the ability to recognize which tasks should be assigned to whom based on my knowledge of others' personal preferences. Understanding my own skillset was key to identifying when I needed to utilize others' skillsets. I needed to know which areas I was an expert in and, more importantly, which areas I was not. I learned quickly that SMEs were an incredible resource. When I did not understand how to do something, or even where to start, all I had to do was think through my relational inventory of colleagues' and stakeholders' expertise and knowledge. Once I identified who was best to guide me on the problem I was facing, I approached that person as the SME and asked for their opinion. It was so much easier than trying to learn everything myself or basing my work approach off an educated guess.

Another aspect of building a relational inventory included examining "pain points" others felt in the work I led. For example, if I constantly found myself re-explaining the same process, I knew I needed to identify where the problem was occurring, which meant asking myself what the root cause was and whether it was a pattern across other tasks. If the root cause traced back to unclear communication that caused confusion among my stakeholders, I had to ask myself what else I communicated that could have confused people. More importantly, I had to identify what about my communication style was confusing so I could improve my skillset and fix the root cause of the problem. Alternatively, if the root cause of the confusion was that one of the steps in the process I outlined did not make good business sense, I needed to know that as well. That meant I needed to find the SME on the process to help me ensure it was robust. To identify the root cause, I asked why it was happening. That was the proper way to learn root causes, and it typically involved me picking up on non-verbal cues and then asking stakeholders in a meeting what concerns they had and why. Although this approach took more effort and time initially, it saved me pain and re-work down the road. It was important for me to take the time to create less pain in my day-to-day by putting in the effort it took to improve something before it snowballed.

The best way to identify a root cause was to actively seek feedback. The best way to resolve it was to utilize my relational inventory – to go to a person that I knew was the SME, or someone who had the skillset I hoped to acquire and learn from them. It was what I had done in the early days of my consulting career without even realizing it. When Jill asked me to set up meet and greets with consultants during my first few weeks, I didn't realize I was interviewing SMEs. I was learning from the experts how to be a good consultant and taking their lessons on how to refine and grow my approach and skillset, and applying it to the challenge I was facing – demonstrating my worth and value as a new employee.

The biggest benefit I reaped from taking relational inventory was the ability to identify mentors. In order to keep a soft copy of relational inventory in my head that listed the skillsets, preferences, and traits of those around me, I had to observe people. Through my observations, I was able to identify people who I respected and admired, people whose thought processes, solutions, and techniques differed from my own. Those were the people who I wanted to learn from. I always tried to have two to three mentors who worked in my field. They had to be in my field because it meant they spoke my language and understood how to navigate the same landscape I was learning. I observed people to identify mentors, but also listened to what others said about their brand. I picked those who had built a brand I wanted to emulate and who offered a different way of thinking than my own. I approached them first to see if they would be interested in serving as a mentor by laying out expectations. I asked if I could meet with them by phone or for lunch or coffee once a month to discuss my goals and obstacles. I would drive the conversation by picking the topics, but the purpose was to pick their brain by getting advice and coaching. Finding mentors and being diligent and disciplined about how I picked them was the number one thing that helped me personally evolve and improve. My mentors, Jill and Stanley, helped guide me along my career path. They gave me advice I had never heard before that I wasn't sure would work, and I blindly trusted them. I tried out the techniques they suggested, first by doing meet and greets and remembering the mantra "you don't know what you don't know." When it worked, I opened my mind a little more and continued to follow their advice on how to build a brand I could be proud of, try new approaches that grew my skills as a professional and an individual, and proactively seek ways to evolve and grow. Jill and Stanley were like the headlights on the vehicle I was driving down a long and dark road of ambiguity. I still could've driven the vehicle through the dark without them, but it would have been much more terrifying and taken a lot longer. I definitely would not have been able to see the road ahead as easily. A colleague once told me that they thought I was a very wise person. While I loved the compliment, I wasn't sure I understood it. I asked what they meant. The colleague told me their definition of wisdom was the ability to learn from others. I bought into that definition because I knew that, of everything I had done in my career to push myself to be and do better, the best thing I ever did was to find and listen to mentors like Jill and Stanley. Listening to their experiences and following their advice saved me the time, effort, and pain that would've taken years to learn on my own. Their wisdom was my guiding light, and I will always look back on the journey they helped me navigate with gratitude and pride.

Prioritize the time it takes to stop and inventory assets, resources, relationships, and reputation. The best way to know what assets you own and which resources are available is to be able to quickly access them. That requires putting in the effort to learn and document everything, including advice and knowledge you acquire, and to organize and catalog your intellectual property. Know where and how to access your past experiences, templates, and tools. Use them to create a consistent experience for the people who interact with you. Allow yourself to build off what you have already done and the knowledge you have already gained so you can propel yourself to the next level. Combine your toolkit and resources with the practice of taking relational inventory, in terms of skillsets, experts, workstyles, communication preferences, and verbal and non-verbal feedback on your performance. It will help you become more cognizant of how you and those around you are perceived. Self-awareness and the ability to tune into your work environment is what will differentiate you from the pack. It will allow you to navigate the business world and your day-to-day job with grace and clarity. It is how you pay homage to your past-self for being committed to growing and refining, and how you set your future-self up for success.

Finally, take inventory on the lessons you learn and revisit them by dedicating time and mindfulness to a self-inventory practice. Congratulate yourself for how far you've come. Think about where you used to be and how much you have grown. Collect your lessons learned by reflecting on the past and identifying how you would change your approach or better manage a stakeholder or communication. Reflect on who your mentors are, who you respect most and why, what advice you receive, and how it impacts you. Think about the observations you make regarding other people's behaviors and what you learn from them, good or bad. Documenting your lessons learned and taking time to review and reflect on them will be one of the most valuable and critical exercises you ever complete in your career. These will become your most treasured assets. Open your mind and allow new ideas to enter. Be receptive to new approaches and ways of thinking; never be afraid to try something different or take a risk. As you progress through your career, you will find that your journey is less about your accomplishments and more about who you become in the process of achieving them.

Chapter Summary

Lesson	How to Implement	When to Implement
Take Inventory	• Schedule check-ins with yourself to reflect on where you have been, where you are going, and where you want to be • Document everything, especially meeting notes and action items, and organize them so they are easily accessible • Scrub and save the intellectual property you create and acquire throughout your career • Educate yourself on your company's free resources and use them • Identify and track people's skillsets, traits, and preferences; use them to build your relational inventory • Be aware of how you are perceived by others; pay attention to things like tone, disinterest, and sudden change of topic • Find the root cause behind "pain points" that others feel when working with you	• At the beginning and end of a new initiative or project you take on • As a quarterly or semi-annual career best practice • In presentations and meetings • When disagreements or misunderstandings occur or a previously agreed upon plan or decision changes

- Leverage your relational
  inventory to identify and
  work with mentors who can
  guide and teach you

Glossary

Term	Definition	Example Sentences
Action Item	A documented event, task, or activity that needs to take place.[1]	I captured the action items from the meeting and will send them out with the minutes we distribute. Who can own this action item?
Ask	To say or write something in the form of a question, in order to get information.[2]	I have an ask for everyone in this meeting to send me their feedback by end of day. I need to clarify the ask before agreeing to own the action.
Deliverable	A tangible or intangible good or service produced as a result of a project that is intended to be delivered to a customer.[3]	We need to define the deliverables required to complete the project. This deliverable will need to go through the defined review and approval process.
Dependency Dependencies Dependent	The relationship of separate but interdependent organizational units. Delineates the direction of ordering elements based	The Legal and Compliance teams have dependencies on one another that must be mapped out before we can understand the full impact. Three different teams co-

	on common objectives or similarities of the task.[4]	manage our supply chain process, each is dependent on the other to complete their steps within the process.
Direct Report	An employee whose position at work is directly below that of another person, and who is managed by that person.[5]	The manager has 15 direct reports. The Executive has a team of direct reports who are working together to identify the right solution.
Intranet	A system of connected computers that works like the internet and allows people within an organization to communicate with each other and share information.[6]	Check the intranet to see if they have templates or examples of change management plans we can use. The company intranet contains org charts and a glossary of commonly used internal acronyms.
Mitigation Mitigate Mitigated	The reduction of something harmful or the reduction of its harmful effects.[7]	For every risk we identified, we needed to clarify the associated mitigation. We have mitigated the risk by removing some language from the training.
Onboard Onboarded Onboarding	To go through procedures to effectively integrate (a new employee) into an organization or familiarize	All new hires will complete onboarding for the first few weeks of their job. This role will require one

	(a new customer or client) with one's products or services.[8]	week of training before the person will be considered fully onboarded to the team.
Pain Points	Something that is a recurring source of trouble, annoyance, or distress.[9]	There are several pain points within this one process. Customers report a variety of pain points with the user experience.
Parking Lot	A meeting management technique used to keep a conversation on-topic without losing good ideas that are not related to the current topic. It is a list of the off-topic items.[10]	Let's review the list of parking lot items captured in the last meeting. While the idea was a great one, it wasn't applicable to the conversation, and therefore lived in the parking lot.
Project Postmortem	A process usually conducted at the conclusion of a project to determine which parts of the project were successful or unsuccessful. Project post-mortems are intended to inform process improvements, mitigate future risks, and promote iterative best practices.[11]	The Project Postmortem will be conducted within 30 days of project completion. Who will attend the Postmortem session next week?
Risk	Factors that may	There is a potential risk to

	jeopardize the success of a project or achieving a goal.[12]	the timeline due to the complexity of implementing the new software system. The risk outweighs the benefit, and, therefore, we will not move forward with the project.
Stakeholder	An individual, group, or organization who may affect, be affected by, or perceive itself to be affected by a decision, activity, or outcome of a project.[13]	I start my project assignments by determining who the key stakeholders are that will require status updates. If we change the process, then we'll need to determine which stakeholders will be most impacted and inform them before the transition takes place.
Subject Matter Expert (SME)	A person with a high-level of knowledge or skill relating to a particular subject or activity.[14]	We need to identify a SME who can help us understand what this process will entail. After consulting a few SMEs, we've realized that we need to incorporate additional time for the implementation phase of this work.
Swag	Products branded with a logo or slogan and	Each new hire is provided with a goodie bag – filled

	distributed to promote a brand, corporate identity, or event.[15]	with swag to decorate their office or take home. To help build excitement around the launch, we will purchase swag and distribute to all employees.
Thought Leader	Someone who, based on their expertise and perspective in an industry, offers unique guidance, inspires innovation, and influences others.[16]	She was seen as a thought leader within the department. I listened carefully to the conversation among the team, wondering who, if anyone, was a thought leader.

Endnotes

1. "Action Item." *Wikipedia: The Free Encyclopedia*, Wikimedia Foundation Inc., 14 October 2019, 16:20 (UTC), en.wikipedia. org/wiki/Action item. Accessed 8 May 2021.
2. Ask." *Oxford Advanced Learner's Dictionary*, Oxford University Press, 2021, oxfordlearnersdictionaries.com/us/definition/en glish/ask_1. Accessed 8 May 2021.
3. "Deliverable." *Wikipedia: The Free Encyclopedia*, Wikimedia Foundation Inc., 4 November 2018, 20:21 (UTC), en.wikipedia.org/wiki/Deliverable. Accessed 8 May 2021.
4. "Organizational Dependencies." *CEOpedia*, Management Online., 1 September 2020, 7:39, https://ceopedia.org/index. php/Organizational_dependence. Accessed 8 May 2021.
5. "Direct Report." *Cambridge Dictionary*, Cambridge University Press, 2021, dictionary.cambridge.org/us/dictionary/english/ direct-report. Accessed 8 May 2021.
6. "Intranet." *Cambridge Dictionary*, Cambridge University

Press, 2021, dictionary.cambridge.org/us/dictionary/english/intranet. Accessed 8 May 2021.

7. "Mitigation." *Wikipedia: The Free Encyclopedia*, Wikimedia Foundation Inc., 28 April 2021, 2:54 (UTC), en.wikipedia.org/wiki/Mitigation. Accessed 8 May 2021.

8. "Onboard." *Oxford Lexico*, Lexico.com, 2021, https://www.lexico.com/en/definition/on-board. Accessed 8 May 2021.

9. "Pain Point." *Merriam-Webser.com Dictionary*, Merriam-Webster, merriam-webster.com/dictionary/pain%20point. Accessed 8 May 2021.

10. "Project Parking Lot." *Project Management Wiki*, Fandom, project-management.fandom.com/wiki/Parking lot. Accessed 8 May 2021.

11. "Project Postmortem." *Lucidmeetings.com*, Second Rise LLC, 2021, lucidmeetings.com/glossary/post-mortem-meeting. Accessed 8 May 2021.

12. "Risk Analysis." *Wikipedia: The Free Encyclopedia*, Wikimedia Foundation Inc., 26 April 2021, 21:30 (UTC), en.wikipedia.org/wiki/Risk analysis_(business). Accessed 8 May 2021.

13. "Project Stakeholder." *Wikipedia: The Free Encyclopedia*, Wikimedia Foundation Inc., 18 April 2021, 22:42 (UTC), en.wikipedia.org/wiki/Project stakeholder. Accessed 8 May 2021.

14. "Expert." *Cambridge Dictionary*, Cambridge University Press, 2021, dictionary.cambridge.org/us/dictionary/english/expert. Accessed 8 May 2021.

15. "Promotional Merchandise." *Wikipedia: The Free Encyclopedia*, Wikimedia Foundation Inc., 8 May 2021, 13:13 (UTC), en.wikipedia.org/wiki/Promotional merchandise. Accessed 8 May 2021.

16. Schooley, Skye. "What is Thought Leadership and Why Does it Matter?" *Business News*, Business.com, 2021, https://www.businessnewsdaily.com/9253-thought-leadership.html. Accessed 8 May 2021

BUSINESS
BOOKS

Business Books

Business Books publishes practical guides and insightful non-fiction for beginners and professionals. Covering aspects from management skills, leadership and organizational change to positive work environments, career coaching and self-care for managers, our books are a valuable addition to those working in the world of business.

15 Ways to Own Your Future

Take Control of Your Destiny in Business and in Life

Michael Khouri

A 15-point blueprint for creating better collaboration, enjoyment, and success in business and in life.

Paperback: 978-1-78535-300-0 ebook: 978-1-78535-301-7

The Common Excuses of the Comfortable Compromiser

Understanding Why People Oppose Your Great Idea

Matt Crossman

Comfortable compromisers block the way of anyone trying to change anything. This is your guide to their common excuses.

Paperback: 978-1-78099-595-3 ebook: 978-1-78099-596-0

Mastering the Mommy Track

Juggling Career and Kids in Uncertain Times

Erin Flynn Jay

Mastering the Mommy Track tells the stories of everyday working mothers, the challenges they have faced, and lessons learned.

Paperback: 978-1-78099-123-8 ebook: 978-1-78099-124-5

The Most Creative, Escape the Ordinary, Excel at Public Speaking Book Ever

All The Help You Will Ever Need in Giving a Speech

Philip Theibert

The 'everything you need to give an outstanding speech' book, complete with original material written by a professional speech-writer.

Paperback: 978-1-78099-672-1 ebook: 978-1-78099-673-8

Small Change, Big Deal
Money as if People Mattered
Jennifer Kavanagh
Money is about relationships: between individuals and
between communities. Small is still beautiful, as the peer-
lending microcredit model shows.
Paperback: 978-1-78099-313-3 ebook: 978-1-78099-314-0

The Failing Logic of Money
Duane Mullin
Money is wasteful and cruel, causes war, crime and
dysfunctional feudalism. Humankind needs happiness, peace
and abundance. So banish money and use technology and
knowledge to rid the world of war, crime and poverty.
Paperback: 978-1-84694-259-4 ebook: 978-1-84694-888-6

Modern Day Selling
Unlocking Your Hidden Potential
Brian Barfield
Learn how to reconnect sales associates with customers and
unlock hidden sales potential.
Paperback: 978-1-78099-457-4 ebook: 978-1-78099-458-1

Readers of ebooks can buy or view any of these bestsellers by
clicking on the live link in the title. Most titles are published
in paperback and as an ebook. Paperbacks are available in
traditional bookshops. Both print and ebook formats
are available online.

Find more titles and sign up to our readers' newsletter at
http://www.jhpbusiness-books.com/
Facebook: https://www.facebook.com/JHPNonFiction/
Twitter: @JHPNonFiction